ACE

THE STORY OF
LT. COL. ACE COZZALIO

Rex Gooch

**Lighthorse Publishing
Company**
Sioux Falls, SD 57104

ISBN: 150864246X
ISBN 13: 9781508642466
Library of Congress Control Number: 2015903256
CreateSpace Independent Publishing Platform
North Charleston, South Carolina

Front cover photo of Ace Cozzalio courtesy of Ray Lane
Image of OH-6 helicopter by Joe Kline Aviation Art
Rear cover photo of Ace and Capt. William Whitworth courtesy of Rex Cozzalio

Dedicated to the Cavalry Troopers Who Wore
"Yellow Scarves and White Stetsons"

Lighthorse Air Cavalry
Vietnam - 1967 to 1972.

TABLE OF CONTENTS

Ace Cozzalio in 1860s Cavalry Uniform – Dong Tam, 1969

Courtesy of Ray Lane

FOREWORD

THIS IS A STORY ABOUT a soldier. Not just any soldier, mind you...an extraordinary soldier whose courageous service is an example to follow whether on the battlefield or in the boardroom. He was a bold and audacious cavalryman whose instincts were those of a warrior. Yes, he got shot down six times over an eighteen-month combat tour in Vietnam, but that was not the result of careless behavior; quite the contrary. He was a skilled Army aviator who used his helicopter as the means by which he would hunt down and destroy the enemy. If he crashed one helicopter, so be it. He'd simply saddle up another one and take it back to the fight until the battle was won.

Brave, aggressive, competent...but above all, he was a LEADER. The kind of leader who earned his position every day by the loyal support he gained from those he led. His physical presence at the point of attack, whether in the rice paddies in the Mekong Delta or at the podium of a classroom in Fort Rucker, made the difference between success and failure.

Rex Gooch offers the reader a carefully researched saga that truthfully presents the history of one of our finest combat leaders from the Vietnam War era. Each event is presented in a most entertaining style that keeps the reader eager to read the next chapter. Take a moment after reading each chapter to ask, "What can I learn from this?" Look for the enduring principles. In doing so, you'll gain the true benefit of this amazing story of a leader who himself was bigger than life.

Tragically, the Army and our nation were denied the full benefit of his potential contribution, as he was taken from us far too early by coronary failure due to the Epstein-Barr virus, a condition over which he had no control. Fighting to the end, we're left with a role model for leadership in the best and most comprehensive sense of that word.

Lift a glass and raise a toast to this heroic American soldier, and then enjoy reading the incredible story of ACE COZZALIO.

Major General Rudolph Ostovich III, U.S. Army (retired)

Author's Note

In this book, I strived to present the truth as accurately as possible. From interviews with people who personally experienced certain events to documents related to those events, I gathered the information and compiled the stories. In many instances, I found multiple sources confirming the stories. In others, I could locate only a single source. When I found conflicting information, I continued my pursuit of the facts until I was confident I had the most reliable source and the most accurate information. If a story presented in this book differs from the recollection of others, it should be kept in mind that many years have passed, memories have faded, and, in some instances, stories have evolved. Nonetheless, this book represents my best effort to accurately portray the extraordinary story of Ace Cozzalio.

Rex Gooch

PREFACE

UPON GRADUATING FROM THE U.S. Army Rotary Wing School in 1971, I received orders for Vietnam. I was young, gung-ho, and looking forward to flying helicopters. My flight instructor had told me stories about his experiences flying for the "1st Cav," and I, too, wanted to fly for the renowned 1st Cavalry Division, whose troopers wore a big yellow patch in the shape of a Norman shield with a black diagonal stripe and a horse's head profile.

Upon arrival in Vietnam, and after a day's stay at the 90th Replacement Company, I was assigned to Lighthorse Air Cavalry, operating in the Mekong Delta. At first I was a little disappointed because it wasn't the 1st Cav. Little did I realize that my momentary sense of disappointment was totally unfounded. I was about to experience the air cavalry in a way I could never have imagined—with Lighthorse!

After a short orientation flight on my first day, I was immediately flying combat missions as copilot (front seat, gunner position) in a Cobra gunship. It didn't take long to realize that Lighthorse was a unique aviation unit, flying to a "different drummer" as the saying goes. The pilots were highly motivated and, most would agree, "tilting to the wild side." Their tactics were developed in the field, and after years of Vietnam combat experience they were highly effective in seeking out and destroying the enemy. I soon learned that Lighthorse had an outstanding combat record and that its troopers were known for their offbeat and unorthodox ways of operating.

As I became accustomed to the cavalry way of flying and the proud traditions of Lighthorse, I heard about a daring pilot who flew for Lighthorse three years before my arrival. His name was Ace Cozzalio, and the stories were not only awe-inspiring but also legendary. Many were so extraordinary that initially I thought they were exaggerated war stories, expanded and embellished after being retold countless times. Not so, I later learned, when I met eyewitnesses who confirmed that the events were factual and, in some cases, even more incredible than the original story.

Most Vietnam helicopter pilots (myself included) had a brazen self-image of a dashing, risk-taking pilot who could fly a helicopter through the midst of enemy fire, skirting treetops, swooping down to skim over rice paddies, and threading the aircraft between trees and other obstacles. With machine guns blazing, we'd take out the enemy along the way, then return to home base unscathed.

While most of us never came close to fulfilling this fantasy, Ace Cozzalio did. Ace was the "real deal." He was bold and self-assured. He walked with a confident swagger that told you he was a "cavalry man." Ace was an extremely talented pilot, performing feats with a helicopter that other pilots would only dream of attempting. And, Ace was a warrior. He relished the idea of flying low level, seeking out and engaging the enemy in a face-to-face shootout while always prevailing.

Years later, while attending Lighthorse reunions, I continued to hear "Ace stories" and often pondered why they were never documented. Like most true war stories, the participants are humble and don't feel comfortable writing about themselves. Eventually, I decided to take the challenge, gather the stories, and compile them in a single narrative about Ace. Travelling to northern California, I interviewed Ace's brother, Rex, and met his mother, Jan. I was fortunate to obtain audio recordings of Ace modestly recounting his

Vietnam adventures to a friend. Then I contacted the Lighthorse pilots and crewmembers who served with Ace and gathered many stories. The result is this book, which imparts the stories and tells of Ace's amazing life—a life cut short by illness at age forty-six.

I present these stories to you and hope you enjoy reading about Ace Cozzalio, a true warrior, patriot, highly decorated Vietnam Veteran, and, in his words, "Always a Cowboy."

Rex Gooch
Longknife 23

CHAPTER 1

CRASH AND BURN

SOUTH VIETNAM, NOVEMBER 1968

SWEEPING LOW AND FAST ACROSS the seemingly never-ending rice paddies east of Ben Tre in the Mekong Delta, First Lieutenant Ace Cozzalio is returning to his home base at Dong Tam to rearm and refuel after a successful scouting mission. He is flying the Cayuse OH-6 Light Observation Helicopter (LOH), commonly called "Loach." Having flown the Loach for six months, Ace has become an accomplished Scout pilot, flying at treetop level or lower while searching for the enemy. Through his relentless, aggressive tactics he has earned the reputation of "top scout" in his air cavalry troop, admired and respected by those who fly with him.

Unlike other Scout pilots, Ace flies low level, both to and from the operations area. Always looking for the enemy, Cozzalio believes he can best find targets of opportunity while skimming across the treetops. The element of surprise often works in his favor, as he catches the Vietcong (VC) in the open before they have a chance to hide. If he finds the enemy, he starts working them over with his machine guns until the air mission commander, flying high above in the Command & Control Huey helicopter, gets clearance from higher command (Battalion or Brigade) to proceed with the attack or cease-fire and continue to the mission area.

Ace feels particularly good on this notably beautiful morning. The visibility is unlimited. High above, the bright, blue sky is dotted with billowy white clouds drifting aimlessly above the attractive countryside. The land below is remarkably flat with a patchwork of bright green rice paddies separated by water-retaining dikes and narrow tree lines. The monsoon season has passed and it's now the flood season, when the Mekong River and its tributaries are at their peak and the vast areas of rice paddies are full of water.

Cozzalio, in the right-side pilot's seat when viewed from inside the cockpit, cruises along at eighty knots (ninety-two mph) airspeed and about thirty feet altitude. His crew chief, who also functions as machine gunner, sits in the left seat with his machine gun pointed out the open doorway, always ready in case they take enemy fire. After many minutes of uneventful flight, Ace decides to take a break, letting his crew chief fly the aircraft.

The crew chief sets his machine gun aside and inserts his temporary cyclic stick (which controls lateral flight) into the empty socket positioned low between his legs. Grabbing the cyclic stick with his right hand and the collective pitch stick (which controls vertical flight) with his left hand, he takes the aircraft controls and says, "I've got it."

"You've got it. Maintain the current heading and altitude and don't do anything tricky," Ace says with a grin.

Then he leans back and relaxes, resting his right foot in the open door frame. Casually looking down through the chin bubble, Cozzalio watches the rice paddies stream by in a green blur beneath the fast-moving Loach. His mind wanders away from the task at hand. He thinks, "What a beautiful country. It's a crying shame there is a war going on here. Maybe I'll return someday under better circumstances."

Warwagon One-Zero, You're on Fire

Suddenly, his daydream is disrupted by a loud *BLAM, BLAM, BLAM* as their Loach takes hits from a .51-caliber antiaircraft gun firing from the tree line on their left. Ace grabs the controls, keys the mic (radio microphone), and yells, "TAKING HITS." Instinctively, he leans the cyclic stick between his legs to the left to bank toward the gun, in hopes of returning fire. Nothing happens—he cannot control the fast-moving aircraft. Apparently one of the rounds severed control rods in the rotor system, and other rounds hit in the engine compartment.

First Lieutenant Marvin Fuller, flying the Command & Control Huey at eight hundred feet altitude, looks down and sees smoke billowing from Ace's Loach. He calls on the troop's "push" (FM radio frequency), "Warwagon One-Zero, you're on fire." He banks slightly left and dives the Huey down to follow behind Ace's smoking aircraft. As he closes in on the Loach, it pops up sixty to seventy-five feet, changes direction, and starts descending.

Ace calls out, "I've lost all cyclic control," as the disabled Loach continues its erratic flight.

The crew chief unbuckles his seat belt and announces on the intercom, "I'm getting out."

Cozzalio answers loudly, "Stay with the aircraft—you're safer onboard."

Ignoring Ace's command, the crew chief disconnects the commo cord from his helmet and turns to the left, swinging his feet out the door. Grabbing the doorframe with both hands, he jumps out. Plummeting about thirty feet into the flooded rice paddy below, he impacts with a huge splash.

Fuller, flying behind the Loach, sees the crew chief jump from the left side of the aircraft. He adjusts his course to follow behind the erratic OH-6 and calls, "Warwagon One-Zero, hang in there—I am right behind you."

The sudden change in the center of gravity causes the errant Loach to veer to the right. Ace attempts to counter the movement by leaning to the left, but it is too little, too late. The Loach continues to swing right, headed for the ground.

Then Ace calls, "I'm gonna ride it in."

ROLLED, JUST LIKE AN EGG

As the uncontrollable aircraft continues to its obvious demise, Ace keys the mic again and says, "Lord, I take back all those bad things I said about ya." Then the helicopter noses in, hitting hard. Years later Ace recalls, "The Loach hit in the rice paddy and rolled, just like an egg. When it stopped, I was upside down with fire behind me."

Restrained by his safety harness, Ace hangs inverted, looking out of what little remains of the busted Plexiglas bubble. "I could feel the flames and fire and could see the damn grenades laying all over the place." His mind races: Grenades and fire—not a good combination. Panic sets in. He knows he has to get out quickly.

With his body weight straining against the safety harness, he cannot release his lap buckle. In this upside-down position, the seat belt inertia reel locked the safety belts, preventing them from extending. Instinctively, Ace grabs for the inertia release lever on the left side of his seat cushion and cannot locate it. His helmet commo cord is tangled, preventing him from turning his head to the left. He quickly removes his helmet and turns to see the release. Grabbing the handle, he gives it a quick pull and promptly falls, resulting in a gash on the back of his head as he hits the top of the inverted cockpit.

Meanwhile, Fuller flares the Huey nose-upward to slow down and comes to a momentary three-foot hover about seventy-five feet in front of the crash. He lowers the collective pitch control with his left hand, and the skids settle into the shallow water and mud of the rice paddy. Fuller quickly rolls the throttle to flight idle and looks over to see Cozzalio hanging upside down with a roaring fire behind him. Fuller said later, "Just as I start to go help Ace, he falls down and crawls out. Our crew chief runs over to help him. As the two walk toward the Huey, I can see the collar on Ace's jungle fatigue shirt is smoking."

MEDEVAC

Cozzalio climbs through the open cargo door and takes a seat against the rear bulkhead. Fuller rolls the throttle to operating rpm, brings the Huey to a hover, does a pedal turn to the left, and takes off, heading to Dong Tam. "I turn and look back at Ace," Fuller said. "He is white as a sheet of paper and his hair is singed in the back where it wasn't protected by his flight helmet."

While this is happening, another scenario plays out. Ace's wingman, flying his trail, sees the crew chief "bail out." He immediately swings the cyclic control to the right, making a tight right-hand turn, and returns to the jump site. He lands his Loach next to the injured trooper lying in the rice paddy mud. He rolls the throttle to flight idle while his crew chief exits the aircraft to assist the injured soldier.

The dazed crew chief has several injuries and needs prompt medical attention. The pilot exits his aircraft and assists his crew chief in loading the injured trooper into the back seat of the Loach. Then the pilot and crew chief climb back into the OH-6 and lift off, flying rapidly to Dong Tam. On arrival, they land on the 3rd Surgical Hospital helicopter pad, where medics rush to the small helicopter and carefully place the injured crew chief on a gurney. Then they wheel him into the hospital, where he is treated for a broken leg and other injuries.

Fuller, who is several minutes behind the wingman, lands his Huey at the medical pad just as the wingman's Loach is departing.

Again, medics respond quickly, putting Ace on a gurney and wheeling him through the double doors of the hospital. With Ace in good hands, Fuller lifts off and relocates to the refueling pads before heading back to the area where Cozzalio was shot down.

Ace is taken to the emergency room in the hospital. After an evaluation by a doctor, an orderly replaces his uniform with a hospital gown, and he is assigned to a bed for observation. Shortly thereafter, he gathers his senses and feels he is perfectly well. He asks to be released, and the medical staff refuses. That doesn't deter Cozzalio; he slips out of the hospital wearing only the hospital gown, open in the back, and cloth slippers. Slowly and cautiously, he makes his way down the gravel road, wincing as the sharp rocks poke through the bottom of the flimsy slippers and impale his feet.

RETURN TO THE BATTLE

Eventually, Ace arrives at the officer barracks, where he dons another set of jungle fatigues and boots. Having escaped the confines of the hospital, he grabs a flight helmet and heads for the Operations Center. On the way, he finds a crew chief and together they check out another Loach.

Meanwhile, Fuller and the Cav Team (two Cobra gunships and two Loaches), now rearmed and refueled, return to the area where Ace was shot down. "By the time we arrive you could put the remains of Ace's burned Loach in a teacup," said Fuller. "We work the area for about an hour and are ready to terminate the mission when we look up and here comes Ace in a Loach, ready to resume the action."

By the time Cozzalio arrives, the Cav Team has taken out the enemy antiaircraft gun and made a thorough Cobra gunship assault on the area, destroying several bunkers in the tree line. Ace makes a low-level pass over the remains of his burned Loach and flies over the now destroyed antiaircraft gun. He'd hoped to give the VC some payback for downing his Loach. Realizing the battle is over, he calls, "Good work, troop. Let's head back."

THE WARRIOR

Time and time again in the annals of history, the tide of battle turns when a warrior rushes to the front and displays great courage and bravery as he meets the enemy head-on. In the Mekong Delta of South Vietnam, that awe-inspiring soldier is Ace Cozzalio.

In mid-1968, after flying with the air cavalry for six months, Ace is firmly established as a warrior, respected and admired by all who know him. He thrives on the thrill and excitement of battle—his mind and body totally focused on the duty of the moment, finding and destroying the enemy forces.

His flying skills in the small, versatile OH-6 helicopter are uncanny, and his unrelenting pursuit of the enemy is beyond compare. As an example, he is known for his "saw" maneuver, during which he attacks an enemy bunker head-on while firing the aircraft's minigun, then backs his helicopter slightly upward, drops the nose, and attacks again and again, decimating the bunker and the enemy combatants inside.

Self-confident and charismatic, Cozzalio is a natural-born leader. With a "follow me" attitude, he is consistently in the forefront of battle and he never asks others to do what he wouldn't do himself. A creative problem-solver, he is best in situations where rapid decisions and initiative are needed—a significant attribute on the field of battle. He is quick to react in dangerous combat situations, yet remains calm and self-possessed in his actions. His exemplary deeds inspire confidence in those around him and loyalty in those he commands.

And, Ace is a maverick, seldom following the tried and true, instead carving his own unique path in his persistent pursuit of excellence. In a unique connection to the horse cavalry soldiers of the past, he creates a modern day "cavalry image" that instills a high level of esprit de corps and personal pride among his fellow cavalry troopers—a pride that continues to this day.

In Cozzalio's eighteen-month tour in Southeast Asia, he is shot down by enemy gunfire six times, not counting the numerous times his helicopter is deemed unflyable due to combat damage. In recognition of his bravery and courage on the field of battle, Ace is awarded every medal of valor beneath the Medal of Honor, including fourteen awards ranked higher than his forty-eight Air Medals.

In subsequent years, Cozzalio has a brilliant military career, commanding a cavalry troop in the United States, an attack aviation company in Germany, and a training battalion at the U.S. Army Aviation School. Having attained the rank of lieutenant colonel, he is recognized as one of the Army's most gifted officers— said to be a future senior leader of the Army. Unfortunately, Ace is diagnosed with a heart problem and medically discharged, cutting his career short after twenty years of service. Seven years later, at age forty-six, Ace valiantly fights another battle, but, this time, victory is not to be his. He passes away after undergoing a heart transplant procedure.

This is the incredible story of Ace Cozzalio—courageous warrior, highly skilled helicopter pilot, and bold cavalryman. But it is also the story of the gallant troopers of Lighthorse Air Cavalry— the pilots and crewmembers who daily strapped into their helicopters and went out to face the enemy in the unforgiving conditions of the Mekong Delta in South Vietnam.

CHAPTER 2

CALIFORNIA COWBOY

BORN IN 1946, ALAN "ACE" Cozzalio grew up on the family ranch, riding his horse, Cody, over the magnificent mountains and valleys of Siskiyou County, California. Overlooking the Klamath River Valley, this 350-acre ranch gave Ace (his family called him Ace) and his two younger brothers, Glen and Rex, ample opportunity to explore and learn from their environment. He loved the wild and rugged terrain of northern California. The ranch culture and cowboy lifestyle were a natural fit for Ace.

From a young age, Ace kept busy helping around the ranch, doing chores and driving a tractor by age nine. But most of all, Ace was a cowboy. He loved horses and spent much of his time in the saddle. He and his horse were inseparable. They traveled the countryside, with Ace imagining himself as one of his favorite western stars: Tom Mix, Gene Autry, or Roy Rogers. On beautiful mornings, it was not unusual for Cody to stick his head through the open kitchen window, looking for Ace as if he wanted to head out on their next adventure.

Ace and Cody
Courtesy of Rex Cozzalio

When asked what the boys did for fun, Ace's youngest brother, Rex, replied: "We did the typical things that kids on a ranch do, like jumping from the thirty-foot haymow into a stack of hay. But the most fun was floating down the Klamath River. Ace, Glen, and I would take inner tubes several miles upriver and float down to Hornbrook, a distance of about seven miles. Once there, we had a special treat. We went to T. Jones Mercantile Store and bought candy. Then we walked back to the ranch."

Undoubtedly, the ranch lifestyle strongly influenced Ace's development. But more importantly, he had two people in his life who played a very important role in the shaping of his character: his mother and his grandfather.

MOM, JAN

Ace's mother, Jan, was a huge influence on him, especially in the development of his tenacity and pursuit of excellence. Raised during the Depression era, Jan was ingrained with a fierce sense of independence, ingenuity, responsibility, and confidence. She believed there was nothing you could not do if determined enough—traits she acquired from her parents. Through his mother's influence, Ace certainly assimilated his "never give up" and "nothing we can't do" attitude. This mind-set is reflected in his favorite saying: "Make no small plans. They have no magic to move men's souls"—a quote also used by Winston Churchill.

Jan Protsman earned several degrees in addition to her Ph.D. and taught at all levels, including college. Jan was teaching when she learned that her fiancé had been killed during World War II. This was devastating for Jan, but she persevered. Sometime later, she met George Carlisle, also a soldier, who had served in WWII as an Army staff sergeant. Jan and George got married and settled in Alturas, California. They opened a jewelry store, with George doing watch repair, and later relocated the store to Westwood, California. On August 19, 1946, they had a son and named him Alan Ace Carlisle. Several years later, Jan and George divorced, but parted as friends.

Afterward, Mel Cozzalio, a logger and millworker, came into Jan's life. Mel and Jan married, and while residing in Westwood, California, Ace's brother, Glen, was born. In 1950, they relocated to the Protsman family ranch near Hornbrook, California (just south of the Oregon border), and moved into the original ranch house, a large one-room cabin near Jan's parents' home. From this location, Jan could continue her education at Ashland, Oregon, and teach at Yreka High School. Mel worked as a logger and also helped with the ranch. It was there that Ace's brother, Rex, was born. Sometime later, Mel became a deputy sheriff for Siskiyou County.

Jan was also a talented artist and excelled in painting portraits and landscapes. She was a founding member of the Portrait Society of America and the Pastel Society of America. She had showings across the nation and gained considerable recognition for her work. Continuing her pursuit of personal growth, Jan obtained her Juris Doctorate after starting a real estate office. It is apparent that Ace inherited much of his determination and ambition from his mother.

"Gramp"

Ace's role model and hero in life was his grandfather, Alfred Ace Protsman, nicknamed "Slim." Born in 1897, Slim had an eighth-grade education, considered good for that time. But more importantly, Slim constantly expanded his knowledge by reading. He read the dictionary, encyclopedias, and the Bible, quoting them often in conversation. He was a self-taught gold prospector, assayer, trapper, blacksmith, woodworker, plumber, electrician, mechanic, and rancher.

The three boys called their grandfather "Gramp." Working side by side with Gramp, Ace learned horsemanship, carpentry, mechanics, and ranching. And, like Gramp, he had an unending thirst for knowledge. But above all else, his grandfather's principled moral code and zeal for life shaped Ace's character. This steadfast sense of right and wrong combined with his Gramp's inherent enthusiasm for life were significant attributes contributing to Ace's success.

Early on, Gramp provided Ace with his first glimpse of the mounted cavalry when he bought him a used McClellan U.S. Cavalry saddle at auction. Slim bought the saddle, not because of its cavalry connection but because it was cheap. Nonetheless, Ace imagined himself "riding with the cavalry," and this surely influenced his later life in the air cavalry.

Another influence was his grandfather's service as an Army sergeant in World War I. Serving with the 269th Aero Squadron in France, Slim was an aircraft mechanic. With great interest, Ace and his brothers listened to their grandfather's stories of meeting General "Black Jack" Pershing and working on Eddie Rickenbacker's airplane. On special occasions, Gramp would unroll a piece of aircraft canvas painted with the renowned "Hat in the Ring" emblem of the 94th Aero Squadron. This iconic insignia was salvaged from one of the fighter biplanes in Rickenbacker's unit while flying with the American Expeditionary Forces. Through these stories, Ace got his first glimpse of military life and aviation. (Note: Gramp later gave the "Hat in the Ring" emblem to Ace. He carried it with him on all military assignments.)

Alfred Ace Protsman
Basic Training Photo – 1917
Courtesy of Rex Cozzalio

ACE THE WARRIOR

In elementary school, Ace was a skinny kid, smaller than his peers. Because he was somewhat shy and not very assertive, he was an easy target for bullying. Determined not to let others take advantage of him, he learned to box, to stand up for himself, and, through his mother's influence, to *never* give in. Before long, he was either winning his confrontations with bigger kids or fighting to a draw, with his opponent regretting taking on this feisty youngster. By the time he was in high school and even before he had attained his full height of six feet, two inches, there was no bullying; instead he gained great confidence and made many friends. This "warrior attitude" became an integral part of Ace and had a significant impact on his military career.

ALAN TO ACE

From the time Ace was a toddler, he was always known as Ace, even though his given name was Alan. Ace was a fitting name for this talented, rambunctious youngster, even more so as he became older. And, the name was a connection to his grandfather since they shared the same middle name. At age eleven, he legally changed his surname from Carlisle to Cozzalio and later, while serving in the Army, he changed his name to Ace Alan Cozzalio.

HIGH SCHOOL—ROCK 'N' ROLL DRUMMER

Having an exemplary record in law enforcement, Mel Cozzalio was offered a job with the California Bureau of Narcotics Enforcement. Mel accepted the offer and the Cozzalio family moved from the ranch to Sacramento, California, when Ace was a sophomore in high school.

The move to California's capital city distanced Ace from his cowboy lifestyle, so he turned to another passion: music. He liked the Beatles and other rock bands popular at the time. Ace learned to play the drums, a passion he maintained his entire life. Like other endeavors, he set his sights high. He decided he wanted to be a rock star, and he and several friends started a band. Their music was popular with the rock 'n' roll crowd, and they were invited to play at school dances and other teen gatherings.

In high school, Ace had many friends. He was good-natured, with a boyish charm that resonated among his companions. But beyond that, Ace had a natural charisma that inspired loyalty—a trait that followed him throughout his later military career and contributed to his success as a leader.

Before graduating from high school, Ace worked part-time as a cook at the International House of Pancakes (IHOP). Motivated to excel, he soon became lead line chef. To celebrate his success, Gramp made him a special long-handled pancake flipper, with his name engraved on the handle. Ace graduated from Mira Loma High School in 1964 and, having risen to assistant manager, appeared to be on his way to becoming the IHOP manager. Then he received an official letter in the mail—his draft notice.

U.S. ARMY

Not wanting to let anyone decide his destiny, Ace went to the local recruiter and joined the Army in February 1966. This proved to be a good decision for Ace. He excelled at Basic Training and was offered the opportunity to attend Officer Candidate School (OCS). It seemed the character traits he acquired from his family surfaced and were instrumental in Ace's success in the Army. After graduation from OCS as a 2nd lieutenant in the Armor Branch at Fort Knox, Kentucky, he applied for and was approved to attend Army Aviation School.

Flying helicopters was a natural fit for Ace—his quest for knowledge, excellent eye-hand coordination, and instinctive abilities made Ace a talented pilot. Eight months later, he graduated from the U.S. Army Rotary Wing Training Course on October 24, 1967, earned his Army Aviator Wings, and received orders for his first duty assignment. Like most newly minted helicopter pilots of the time, Ace was headed for Vietnam.

CHAPTER 3

LIGHTHORSE

SECOND LIEUTENANT ACE COZZALIO ARRIVED in Vietnam on December 1, 1967, and was assigned to D Troop, 3rd Squadron, 5th Cavalry, whose base camp was located at Camp Bearcat, a military installation twenty miles east of Saigon. Upon his arrival at Bearcat, he reported for duty with D Troop and learned that 3-5 Cavalry (3rd Squadron of the 5th Cavalry Regiment) was known as the "Bastard Cav." Ace probably didn't realize it at the time, but this fateful assignment to the Bastard Cav would align with his maverick nature and enable him to excel in ways he never imagined.

BASTARD CAV

The 3rd Squadron of the 5th Cavalry Regiment was attached to the 9th Infantry Division as their reconnaissance unit. Since 3-5 Cavalry was a standalone cavalry unit attached to an infantry division and not part of a cavalry division, they were called the Bastard Cav. (Note: In the Korean War, 3-5 Cav was a regiment of the 1st Cavalry Division.)

5th Cavalry

The pilots and crewmembers of D Troop readily identified with the Bastard Cav image.

Not unlike the Black Sheep Squadron of World War II, D Troopers pushed the limits of their machines and their flying abilities, and at times challenged the rules of engagement when chasing the enemy. This image of rogue, renegade, and rebel appealed to D Troopers and, for Ace Cozzalio, it was soon to be a perfect match.

DELTA 9—THE 9TH INFANTRY DIVISION RADIO BROADCAST

In January 1969, "Delta 9," the weekly radio report of the 9th Infantry Division, interviewed several D Troop pilots. The lead-in for that broadcast gave an overview of the air cavalry.

(Rousing music lead-in with bugles sounding)

When the word *cavalry* is heard, most people imagine men like General George Custer in a dark blue uniform leading a hundred mounted men in a cavalry charge. There's a new type of cavalry charge happening daily in the Vietnam War. The men are dressed in olive green fatigues and flight helmets. The charge is the sound of helicopter Gunships roaring over the nipa palm and rice paddies of Vietnam with fire-breathing rockets and rapid-fire miniguns blazing.

(Sound of miniguns and machine guns roaring)

This cavalry is the air cavalry, or better known to ground troops as simply "the Cav." The Cav consists of a breed of fighting man unique among Americans troops. The pilots fly the most modern helicopters available, and the small platoons of ground troops are quick to admit that their job is dangerous. That job is finding the enemy, many times a force much larger than their own.

One of the outfits of the air cavalry is Delta Troop, 3rd Squadron, 5th Cavalry. Delta Troop works with the 9th Infantry Division in the Mekong Delta.

MEKONG DELTA

D Troop, in support of the 9th Infantry Division, conducted combat operations throughout IV Corps, the southernmost U.S. Armed Forces–designated quadrant of South Vietnam. IV Corps was essentially the Mekong Delta.

For Ace, the Mekong Delta terrain was entirely different from the mountains and valleys of northern California where he grew up. And, it was unlike the wooded hills and valleys of the country-side he encountered stateside in Army flight school.

Here, the landscape was flat with an elevation of less than ten feet above sea level and the climate was hot and humid. Needless to say, it required a certain amount of acclimation in terms of living conditions and adjustments in flying procedures. The very nature of the flat terrain made helicopters easy to spot. To avoid small arms fire, most aircraft flew at 1,500 feet or higher. Ace, however, chose be "on the deck," flying low and fast.

The Mekong Delta (see map) was formed by the mighty Mekong River entering Vietnam from Cambodia and spreading southeast through many tributaries and canals to eventually flow into the South China Sea. Along the way, this massive river system deposited its silt to build flat, fertile land. Here palm trees grew tall, and the vegetation spread thick and fast. It was comprised mostly of mangrove swamps and vast areas of rectangular rice paddies separated by dikes.

The continual transition from open rice paddies to dense vegetation and back again made the Mekong Delta a treacherous place to fly. In his book titled, *Outlaws in Vietnam,* David Eastman commented, "In the Delta, one went from relative safety to immediate [enemy] contact in the blink of an eye, and we helicopter pilots were all used to that fact."[1]

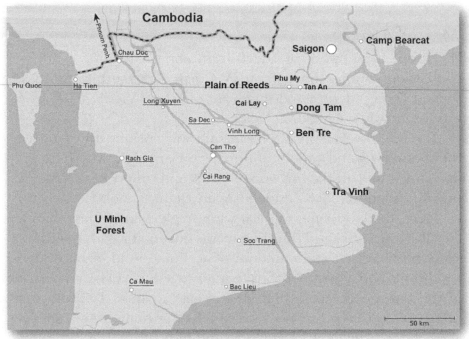

Mekong Delta—IV Corps

Transportation was predominantly by water on the countless interlocking canals, both natural and manmade, which crisscrossed the Delta. Using sampans (long, slender, flat-bottomed, wooden boats) as their primary means of travel, the Vietnamese people traversed the waterways with ease, taking their rice and goods to market in the local villages.

During the Vietnam War, the battle for control of the Mekong Delta was hotly contested. Two-thirds of the nation's population lived in the Delta and produced about the same proportion of the country's rice. Whoever controlled the Delta controlled the country's food supply.[2]

D/3-5 AIR CAVALRY—LIGHTHORSE

To fully appreciate Ace Cozzalio's escapades as a "Cav pilot," it is helpful to understand how D Troop, also called D Troop Air, was structured and its primary mode of combat. What follows is an overview of this unique cavalry troop's operations.

Cavalry troops had nicknames, such as "Apache," "Centaurs," and "Blue Ghost." D Troop's nickname was "Lighthorse," a fitting name for a cavalry troop with a heritage going back to the horse cavalry of the late 1800s.

> Lineage: The 5th Cavalry Regiment was constituted in the U.S. Army of the Potomac in 1861 when the 2nd Cavalry (created in 1855) was re-designated in preparation for the Civil War. Fighting for the Union in the Fredericksburg, Chancellorsville, Gettysburg, Shenandoah, and Appomattox campaigns, the regiment had an impressive Civil War record.
>
> Moving west in 1868, the 5th Cavalry fought valiantly in the Indian Wars across Kansas, Oklahoma, Colorado, Wyoming, South Dakota, and Nebraska. During its twenty-two years of frontier service, thirty members of the 5th Cavalry were awarded the Congressional Medal of Honor.[3]

Operating as an independent cavalry troop, Lighthorse developed tactics that set them apart from other air cavalry troops. Their primary combat operation was the search and destroy mission (described later in this book). An essential distinction was a team of two Scout helicopters that flew low, slow, and "in your face" with the enemy. This tactic proved to be highly effective in finding and engaging the Vietcong throughout the Mekong Delta.

Lighthorse was composed of three combat aircraft platoons, one aero-rifle platoon, and a maintenance platoon. The combat aircraft platoons were Scout, Gunship, and Lift. Each platoon had a unique nickname that was used as its radio call sign. The following table can be used as a guide for nicknames and call signs used in this book.

Lighthorse Nicknames and Call Signs				
Platoon	**Aircraft**	**Nickname**	**Call Sign**	**Nos.**
Scout	OH-6A LOH	Scouts	Warwagon	11–19
Lift	UH-1 Huey	Slicks	Longknife	20–29
Gunship	AH-1G Cobra	Guns	Crusader	30–39
Aero-rifle			Doughboy	40–49
Maintenance			Scavenger	50–59
Commanding Officer		CO	Lighthorse	6
Executive Officer		XO	Lighthorse	5

Military communications procedures stated that radio calls begin with the person being called, followed by the caller and then the message. A typical radio call between Warwagon 15 and Crusader 33 would sound like this: "Crusader Three-Three, this is Warwagon One-Five. Cover my right flank." In the field, this radio call would be shortened to: "Three-Three, One-Five. Cover my right flank." And, when the Warwagon Scouts flew low and in harm's way, the radio calls were even more abbreviated: "Three-Three, cover my right flank."

As a cavalry troop, Lighthorse was comparable in size to an infantry company. D Troop's authorized manpower in 1969 was 266 military personnel and twenty-seven aircraft, plus jeeps, trucks, and other support vehicles. The table below shows a breakout of D Troop's authorized personnel and aircraft.

D/3-5 Cavalry TOE (Table of Organization & Equipment) Authorized—Dec 1969[i]			
Personnel		**Aircraft**	
Enlisted Men	216	OH-6A LOHs	10
Officers	14	AH-1G Cobras	9
Warrant Officers	36	UH-IH Hueys	8

WARWAGON SCOUT PLATOON

The Warwagons flew the OH-6A Light Observation Helicopter, nicknamed "Loach." This small, highly maneuverable aircraft flew at treetop level or lower as it searched for the enemy. Because of this advance combat reconnaissance role, the OH-6 was also called a "Scout," and the men flying them were proud to be called Scout pilots. Their mission was not unlike the horse cavalry scouts of the 1860s—forward reconnaissance to locate the enemy. This aircraft and the pilots who flew them are discussed in detail in Chapter 6.

While Ace flew other aircraft, he was first and foremost a Scout pilot. He was adept at flying this small aircraft and savored the "out front" mission, seeking out and attacking the enemy. He was an exceptional OH-6 pilot, experiencing many adventures and near misses described later in this book.

Warwagon OH-6 Loach
Courtesy of Mike Galvin

CRUSADER GUNSHIP PLATOON

In June 1968, D Troop received the new AH-1G Cobra helicopter, nicknamed "Snake." Designed to replace the C Model Huey gunship, the Cobra was the Army's first dedicated attack helicopter. This sleek two-person gunship was fast with a Vne (never exceed) speed of 190 knots (219 mph) and a cruising speed of 150 knots (173 mph). It had stub-wing pylons on each side of the fuselage for attaching an assortment of armament, including 2.75-inch folding-fin rockets and/or wire-guided anti-tank missiles.

Crusader AH-1G Cobra Gunship
Courtesy of Tom Nutting

Two pilots manned the Cobra. The copilot, sitting in the front seat, controlled the steerable nose turret that housed an M134 six-barrel, 7.62-milimeter minigun, capable of firing two thousand or four thousand rounds per minute, and an M-129 forty-millimeter grenade launcher. The pilot, in the rear seat, aimed the aircraft at the target and launched 2.75-inch folding-fin rockets—either high explosive or flechette (2,200 small metal darts) rounds. This deadly aircraft was highly effective in attacking both personnel and mechanized vehicles.

"Flying the Cobra was exhilarating!" wrote Randy Zahn in *Snake Pilot*. "It was fast and incredibly maneuverable; the visibility flying from the front seat was fantastic and in every sense of the word, it was an attack aircraft."[5]

Ace moved from Warwagon Scouts to Crusader Gunships in the last six months of his Vietnam tour. The warrior traits that served him well while flying Scouts made him an aggressive Cobra Gunship pilot with flying skills unmatched by other pilots.

LONGKNIFE LIFT PLATOON

The Longknives flew the UH-1 Utility Helicopter, commonly called "Huey." This iconic helicopter was the recognized workhorse of the Vietnam War. The D Model Huey carried up to six U.S. soldiers with gear, or eight South Vietnamese soldiers. The newer and more powerful H Model, introduced in January 1969, carried up to eight U.S. soldiers with gear or ten South Vietnamese soldiers. A pilot and copilot flew the Huey, supported by a crew chief and door gunner. The crew chief on the left side and gunner on the right side, sitting inside open cargo doors, manned M-60 machine guns.

Longknife UH-1 Huey, aka Slick
Courtesy of Mike Galvin

Hueys were also called "Slicks." This name was derived during the time that Charlie Model Hueys served as gunships and were nicknamed "Guns" or "Hogs." Hueys without rockets were called "Slicks," referring to their lack of heavy armament. This name stuck with the Hueys even after the introduction of the Cobra gunships.

While the Loach and Cobra helicopters served as the war machines for the air cavalry, the versatile Huey was always there for support, whether it was troop insertion, medevac, or crash recovery.

BEST OF THE BEST

Lighthorse had some of the Army's finest pilots. They were highly proficient aviators, and singularly dedicated to the successful completion of their mission. That said, Ace Cozzalio was the best of the best. He was a skilled pilot, a respected leader, and, most of all, a warrior. What follows are some of the most interesting stories about Ace that occurred during his eighteen-month tour in Vietnam.

CHAPTER 4

MEDEVAC TO JAPAN

"The world will be improved only by those who
are willing to follow their own consciences."

—ACE COZZALIO

ACE'S FIRST ASSIGNMENT WAS FLYING Hueys in the Longknife Platoon.
First Lieutenant Rich Petaja, Longknife platoon leader, recalls, "I
liked Ace the moment I met him. He was a cheerful guy who always
had a positive attitude and loved to fly. Hailing from California,
the guys kidded him about being a surfer. I don't think Ace had
ever surfed, but happily went along by saying 'surf's up' to keep the
joke going."

LRRP INSERTION MISSION, DECEMBER 12, 1967
Ace Cozzalio awakens at 0430 hours, puts on his uniform, and grabs
his flight helmet, pistol, and gloves and heads for the Operations
Center (OPS) for today's flight assignment. Ace is a newbie (new
pilot), having been in-country only twelve days. He has flown copilot on four previous missions and is looking forward to today's
flight with Rich Petaja, his platoon leader.

Upon reaching OPS, Ace walks into the heavily fortified building situated near the flight line. Inside, this large single room with no windows is lit by a string of lightbulbs hanging from the ceiling. On the wall is a large map of the Mekong Delta with red grease pencil markings denoting areas of previous enemy contact. Behind the counter are a couple of desks, one for the operations sergeant and another for troop communications. The latter table holds a bank of five radios monitoring 9th Infantry Division and D Troop radio frequencies and a couple of landline telephones used for communications that exceed the range of the radios. For a new pilot, this is exciting, a glimpse into the nerve center of air cavalry operations.

Ace looks around the room and sees Rich Petaja talking to a group of three pilots. As he approaches the group, he overhears Rich talking about today's mission. When Petaja sees Ace approach, he stops in midsentence to introduce Cozzalio as his newbie "peter pilot" (copilot).

After a few new-guy jokes, the discussion continues. Ace learns they are assigned a mission to insert a LRRP team in the dense jungle north of Saigon. The standard procedure is a "single ship" Huey carrying the LRRP team, accompanied by a maintenance/recovery Huey and two Crusader Gunships. The second Huey and gunships orbit several miles away, on call, to provide support and firepower if needed. The key to success for this mission is to fly in fast, drop the LRRPS, and exit quickly—before the enemy can get a sense of their location.

LRRPs, pronounced "Lurps," is an acronym for long-range reconnaissance patrols. Patrolling deep into enemy-held territory, these small, heavily armed reconnaissance teams consist of six infantry soldiers specially trained in "Recondo" tactics. Using stealth, cover, and concealment, the teams perform surveillance and reconnaissance while avoiding contact with enemy forces and the local population. Huey helicopters are used to insert LRRP teams in strategic locations, from where they execute their recon missions, sometimes remaining in the field for weeks at a time.

Today's mission is different. Unlike the Mekong Delta with its rice paddies, dikes, and canals, the insertion area is in the midst of triple-canopy jungle near a suspected enemy base camp. On the previous day, Petaja, accompanied by the LRRP team leader, flew an aerial recon of the area and selected an appropriate landing zone (LZ) from a distance. Not wanting to tip off the enemy of their plans, Rich took great precaution to avoid overflying the LZ.

PREFLIGHT AND STARTUP

As the morning sun is peeking over the horizon, Petaja and Cozzalio meet their crew chief and door gunner at the Huey helicopter parked in an L-shaped sandbag revetment (barricade protecting helicopters from mortars or rockets) on the flight line. After a preflight inspection, the two pilots climb into the cockpit, Cozzalio in the left seat and Petaja in the right seat (as viewed from inside the aircraft). They strap into their seats, put on their helmets, and plug their helmet's commo cord into the aircraft's microphone jack.

At the same time, the crew chief unties the long strap that secures the rotor blade to the tail boom and rotates the rotor blades to the starting position, ninety degrees off the nose.

With Ace reading the checklist, Rich initiates the startup procedure. After checking a number of circuit breakers and switches, he reaches up to the overhead console between the pilot seats and turns the BAT (battery) switch to the "on" position. Then he turns and reaches both hands to the collective pitch control on the left side of his seat. With his right hand, he holds the linear actuator button for ten seconds. With his left hand, he twists the throttle to full open and rolls it back to the idle detent. Pressing the idle detent button, he rolls the throttle a little further to the start position and yells, "Clear?" The crew chief and gunner both respond in unison, "Clear."

Petaja pulls the start trigger on the underside of the collective and the starter motor groans as the engine slowly starts to rotate. A very distinctive clicking sound is heard from the engine compartment as the fuel igniters start sparking, lighting the start fuel as it's sprayed into the combustion chamber. The engine surges to life as a thick cloud of black, sooty smoke emits from the tail pipe of the Lycoming T-53 engine and the air fills with the heavy smell of burning JP4 jet fuel. At 25 percent N_1 speed (first compressor fan in the turbine engine) the rotors are turning, and at 40 percent N_1 the engine runs on its own as Petaja releases the start trigger.

The Huey rocks from side to side as the rotor blades turn slowly at first, then faster and faster. After the exhaust temperature stabilizes, Petaja twists the throttle all the way to full. Using the linear actuator button, commonly called the "beep switch," he bumps the engine rpm up to 6600 and the rotors settle in at 324 rpm. The rotor blades are spinning in sync, and the vibrations calm down to a smooth rhythm. The Huey is ready for flight.

Rich engages the intercom trigger on the cyclic stick and tells Ace, "OK, take the controls and bring the aircraft to a hover. Then slide to the right, away from the revetment."

Ace replies, "I've got it."

Rich replies, "You've got it," and releases the controls to Ace.

Helicopter Flight Controls:

Cyclic—Control stick positioned between the pilot's legs that controls left–right and forward–backward movement of the helicopter. The cyclic control tilts the main rotor disk in the direction of desired movement.

Collective—Control stick on left side of pilot. Lifting the collective increases pitch (angle) in the rotor blades for lift. On the end of the collective is a motorcycle-like grip that controls power to the engine. The collective controls the vertical movement of the helicopter.

Pedals—Foot pedals control the pitch (angle) of the tail rotor. The tail rotor counteracts the torque created by the main rotor blades. Pushing the pedals allows the pilot to adjust for changes in rotor blade torque. Pushing the right pedal turns the aircraft's nose to the right and vice versa.

After receiving clearance from the crew chief and door gunner, Ace slowly lifts the collective pitch control and adds a little left pedal until the Huey is light on its skids. He moves the cyclic in a small circle to get the "feel" of cyclic center to avoid drifting in any direction. He continues slowly, lifting the collective until the skids break free from the ground. Being careful to avoid the sandbag wall on the left side of the aircraft, he brings the Huey to a three-foot hover and slides to the right, away from the revetment.

Petaja calls on the radio, "Bearcat tower, Longknife Two-Six requesting clearance to cross the runway at midfield."

The tower replies, "Two-Six, you are clear to cross."

Ace brings the Huey to a high hover, moves across the runway, and sets down near the LRRP team. The LRRPs grab their backpacks and weapons and climb aboard the Huey.

Meanwhile, two Crusader Charlie Model Huey gunships (pre-Cobra days) and another Longknife Slick have cranked their engines and hovered out of their revetments. They move to positions alongside the runway and set down.

Crusader 32 calls, "Longknife Two-Six, this is Three-Two. I have Crusader Three-Five and Longknife Two-Three ready to roll."

Petaja responds, "Roger that, Three-Two. Our pax [passengers] are aboard, and we are ready."

Rich keys the radio and calls the airfield control tower. "Bearcat tower, this is Longknife Two-Six with a flight of four helicopters, requesting clearance to depart to the west."

The tower responds, "Two-Six, flight of four, clear to depart, runway two four. Winds are three two zero at five knots (six mph). Altimeter setting three zero zero four."

Rich responds, "Roger, three zero zero four," as he reaches to dial in the barometric pressure on the altimeter.

LIFTOFF

Ace lifts the Huey to a hover and moves to the middle of the asphalt runway. After a pedal turn, he pauses for a second and then applies light forward pressure on the cyclic control. The Huey dips its nose, lifts its tail, and starts moving forward. After traveling about fifty feet, the helicopter goes through translational lift (additional lift from the horizontal flow of air across the rotor blades) and starts climbing.

Rich keys the intercom, telling Ace to take a north-northwest heading and climb to 1,500 feet altitude. Monitoring his instruments, Ace sets up a rate of climb at five hundred feet per minute while maintaining his NNW heading. Upon attaining 1,500 feet, he levels off and maintains eighty knots (ninety-two mph) airspeed.

The two Crusader Gunships and the Longknife Huey take off shortly afterward and join Longknife 26 at altitude. Crusader 32 calls, "Two-Six, this is Three-Two. You have a flight of three on your six."

Rich replies, "Roger that, we are one zero mikes [minutes] from our AO [operations area]."

It is 0730 hours, and the morning sun is painting a warm glow over the treetops as they pass over the perimeter of the dense jungle. Several minutes later, Petaja sees the LZ in the distance.

Rich keys the radio and calls, "Crusader Three-Two, hold here while we go in."

Crusader 32 replies, "Roger that, holding here. Holler if you need us." Then the two Crusader Gunships and the maintenance/recovery Huey break to the left, entering a large, oval holding pattern.

Rich places his right hand on the cyclic, triggers the intercom switch, and says, "I've got it," as Ace relinquishes the controls. He lines up his Huey on the LZ and drops to treetop level. Flying at eighty knots (ninety-two mph), he skims above the trees in the direction of the LZ. As he closes on the landing zone, he decreases power and flares the Huey's nose upward to slow the airspeed. Upon reaching the perimeter of the LZ, he drops the nose, lowers the collective, and begins his descent.

THE CRASH

Suddenly, the Huey starts spinning to the right, and Petaja realizes he has lost all pedal control. Apparently, the tail rotor hit something as they passed over the trees along the perimeter of the LZ. Rich lowers the collective pitch control and rolls off the throttle in an attempt to slow the spinning. This, in turn, increases their rate of descent, the disabled Huey falling rapidly. At about fifteen feet above ground, he levels the aircraft and pulls up on the collective in an attempt to slow the descent and cushion the contact with the ground, but it is too late. The Huey hits with a crushing impact in the small landing zone.

After the shock of the crash subsides, Petaja looks over at Ace, who is unconscious. One of the rotor blades slammed down into the cockpit, hitting the top of Ace's flight helmet. The impact forced his head downward, his jaw hitting the heavy "chicken plate" (body armor) he is wearing across his chest. The crushing blow fractured Ace's jaw and knocked him unconscious.

Rich tries to open his door but finds it is jammed shut from the crash. He exits through the broken windshield and rushes to the left side of the aircraft. There he finds that Ace's door is jammed shut, too. Meanwhile, the Huey's turbine engine continues running at high rpm, emitting a high-pitch whining noise. Petaja, fearful the engine might explode or catch fire, tells the crew chief to shut it down while he and the gunner attempt to get Ace out of the mangled cockpit.

Rich is frantically trying to remove the door's hinge pins when the gunner suggests they unlock the seat back and tilt it backwards into the passenger compartment. This works. They drop the seat rearward and remove Ace, who is still unconscious. They carry him away from the crash and lay him on the ground. Slowly he comes to, yet he remains dazed and groggy.

Meanwhile, the crew chief turns the fuel valve off and the engine whines down. In the newfound silence, the LRRP team moves into the jungle and sets up a perimeter defense around the crashed helicopter.

Minutes earlier, Crusader 32 watched as Longknife 26 dropped out of sight in the midst of the jungle. When the Huey didn't reappear, he became worried. He called Longknife 26 several times and got no response.

Sensing something bad has happened, he calls the maintenance/recovery Huey. "Longknife Two-Three, this is Three-Two. I think we have a problem. Head for the LZ to check it out and we will follow on your six."

Rich climbs back into the cockpit and attempts to use the Huey's radios to call for help. The radios are inoperable, apparently damaged in the crash. Going to the front of the aircraft, he pries open the nose compartment, retrieves the PRC-90 survival radio, and broadcasts a Mayday call.

Arriving above the crash site, Longknife 23 answers the call and talks to Petaja.

Both pilots agree; the jungle is so dense around the crash site that there is no suitable area to land. Rich describes Ace's injuries and suggests they call for a medevac.

Crusader 32, monitoring the conversation from high above, places a Mayday call requesting an emergency extraction in the jungle.

RESCUE

At 0825 hours, the control tower at Bien Hoa airfield answers the Mayday call and alerts the Air Force's 38th Rescue and Recovery Squadron. Detachment 6 of the 38th Squadron, call sign Pedro, has two rescue helicopters sitting on the ready ramp adjacent to Bien Hoa airfield. In a matter of minutes, the two helicopters take off, heading east to the crash site about ten miles from Bien Hoa.

About fifteen minutes after making the Mayday call, Petaja looks up to see a bright orange Air Force rescue helicopter hovering high above the jungle canopy. This strange-looking helicopter with two counter-rotating, intermeshing rotor blades is an H-43 Huskie, specially designed for rescue and firefighting. Pedro 97 comes to a steady hover and lowers a Stokes litter down through the opening in the trees. They load Ace into the basket, and the rescue helicopter hoists him upward. Once he is safely aboard, Pedro 97 departs, taking him to the 24th Field Evacuation Hospital at Long Binh, arriving at 0850 hours.[6]

Petaja and his crew remain in the LZ with the crashed Huey for most of the day while the LRRP team continues providing protection for the downed aircrew. Before nightfall, a squad of Lighthorse

Doughboys makes its way to the LZ and escorts the Huey crew through the dense jungle to an open area for helicopter pickup.

The LRRP team remains in the area until a Chinook helicopter arrives to sling load the Huey back to Camp Bearcat. Once the Chinook retrieves the crashed aircraft, the LRRPs strike out to resume their mission in the jungle.

ACE MEDEVACED TO JAPAN

After an in-country medical evaluation, it is determined that Ace needs maxillofacial surgical repairs on his broken jaw. Since those medical services are not available in Vietnam, Ace is medevaced to Yokohama, Japan. Arriving in Japan on December 28, 1968, he is admitted to the 106th General Hospital. It is there that Ace's jaw is wired shut, requiring him to drink liquid meals through a straw.

Cozzalio is assigned to a lively ward of lieutenants in similar circumstances, recuperating from injuries or wounds. Most are ambulatory, able to move about and take care of themselves with minimal assistance. Receiving passes, Ace and several other lieutenants go to Tokyo for the weekend.

Later, Ace writes his mother about seeing the Kabuki Theater and visiting the Tokyo Tower overlooking the city. Initially, the interaction with the other lieutenants and the fascination with Tokyo serves well to pass the time. But soon, boredom sets in and Ace is anxious to return to his troop in Vietnam

On inpatient status for six weeks, Cozzalio is scheduled to have the wires removed in early February prior to his anticipated hospital release on February 9, 1968.

ACE'S RETURN

In mid-January, Ace receives orders for his next duty assignment, Fort Lewis, Washington. Most would be delighted, but not Ace—he wants to return to Vietnam and continue flying with Lighthorse. Not desiring to stick around until his fate is sealed, he packs a small bag and takes a taxi to Yokota Air Force Base.

Having no orders would be a problem for most, but Ace is resourceful. He approaches the crew of an Air Force C-130 cargo plane and convinces them to give him a ride to Vietnam. The Air Force crew most likely thought that anyone crazy enough to want to return to Vietnam deserved a ride.

Arriving in Cam Rahn Bay, Ace catches a flight on a Huey helicopter to U.S. Army Headquarters at Long Binh, about ten miles east of Saigon. There, he looks for a ride back to Camp Bearcat.

BACK AT D TROOP

In early January 1968, First Lieutenant Carl Eisemann joined Lighthorse, flying Hueys in the Longknife Lift Platoon. Being a new guy, he was assigned the duty of gathering Ace's personal belongings and shipping them stateside since no one expected Ace to return. Not having met Ace, Eisemann didn't give it much thought. He boxed up Ace's belongings and shipped them to Fort Lewis, Washington.

In the third week of January, Eisemann flies an "ash and trash" mission transporting GIs, who completed their tour, to Long Binh for out-processing and the flight home. He lands his Huey at the LBJ (Long Binh Junction) helipad.

After the last passenger departs, a tall, lanky guy comes running toward the Huey, throws his bag in the passenger compartment, and announces with clenched teeth, "I'm back."

Eisemann asks, "Who are you?"

The new passenger replies, "I'm Ace." He has no orders and explains he hitched rides with the Air Force back to Vietnam. Eisemann lifts off and returns to Camp Bearcat with Ace on board.

Years later, Rich Petaja recalled the day that Ace unexpectedly walked into the pilot's tent. All eyes were on Ace as he entered and said, "Surf's up."

Ace Is AWOL

At some point, the 106th General Hospital reported Ace as AWOL. Like most government personnel actions, the paperwork was slow, and by the time it got to the 9th Division Headquarters Ace was already flying with D Troop. What happened is uncertain, but evidently someone decided he was doing his job well so they left him alone. Ace got his wish; he stayed with Lighthorse and continued flying helicopters.

CHAPTER 5

HOT WATER

"Imagination can be more important than knowledge."

—ACE COZZALIO

RETURNING TO LIGHTHORSE, ACE DISCOVERS that his belongings were shipped to Fort Lewis, Washington, his supposed new duty assignment. This seemingly doesn't bother Cozzalio, who takes it all in stride. He goes to the supply room and requisitions a cot, bedding, new uniforms, and other equipment. Because his jaw is still wired shut, Ace mumbles somewhat when speaking, but that doesn't slow him down otherwise. He is happy to be back with D Troop and is anxious to return to flying.

A few days later, Ace meets his new hooch mate (roommate), Second Lieutenant Marvin Fuller, who is returning from emergency leave. Several weeks pass when Fuller, who was promoted to first lieutenant, suddenly realizes that Cozzalio, whose date of rank is thirty days before Fuller's, hasn't been promoted. And, to make matters worse, Ace isn't being paid because he has no personnel records. Once again, Ace flashes his classic smile. It doesn't seem to matter to him. Fortunately, Marvin is gracious enough to share his belongings with Ace and loan him money until his records catch up with him.

Four Left Feet

One day, Marvin realizes that Ace has been "borrowing" his shaving kit. He loans him some money to purchase a shaving kit and other personal items at the Post Exchange (PX). Since Fuller had mistakenly acquired two left feet shower shoes, he tells Ace to reach into the big bin at the PX and grab two right feet shower shoes so they will both have a set.

Later, Ace returns from the PX and happily starts unloading his bag. At the bottom, he reaches in and tosses the shower shoes on the floor—two more left feet.

"So, we both had two left feet shower shoes," laughed Fuller. "If the VC were tracking us at Bearcat, it surely had them confused."

The Shower Project

In every military unit, there are a number of "odd jobs" needing to be performed. In an air cavalry troop, most of the personnel are pilots and crewmembers who are busy flying, leaving only a small group of candidates to perform these undesirable jobs. Since Ace is medically grounded from flying, he is an obvious choice. Being assigned to the "odd jobs" frustrates Ace, especially since he yearns to be flying.

In Lighthorse, the Troop's executive officer (XO), an Army captain, maintains a long list of extra duties to be performed in the Troop area. One day the XO calls Ace into his office and gives him the top assignment on his list—hot water for the officers' shower. Until now, the shower consisted of a large bladder of cold water atop a wood-framed tower. A wooden plank fence with a hinged door enclosed the shower area beneath the tower, and a pull chain released cold water from a spigot. Ace's challenge is to build a water heating system that heats the water flowing between the tower and the showerhead.

As always Ace accepts the project with a good attitude, but he is somewhat perplexed since he has no experience in such things. He contacts several people to get ideas and develops a plan. Before long he gathers a large assortment of tools, pipes, fittings, etc., near the base of the shower and starts his construction.

"Day after day, we see Ace working on the shower," said Fuller. "He has lots of pipes, an immersion heater from the mess hall, and a couple of fifty-five-gallon drums. He toils with his shirt off, banging on pipes and sweating profusely. We wave at him as we go to the flight line. Ace waves back and mumbles something in return, his jaw still wired shut."

This scene repeats itself for days on end. It soon becomes an item of discussion and is impacting morale—the officers are anxiously awaiting the day they will have hot showers. Eventually, some wise guy posts a sign on the shower door saying "3 days to hot water," "2 days to hot water," "1 day to hot water" until the much-awaited day arrives.

HOT WATER

"After a busy day in the air, we return on the day of hot water," said Fuller. "Everybody runs to the barracks, grabs their soap on a rope, and, with a towel wrapped around them, lines up at the door of the shower."

Meanwhile, Ace continues working on the hot water machine. "This 'Rube Goldberg' contraption has fire flaming from the bottom and is chugging and smoking, just like a steam engine," said Marvin. "He and one of the crew chiefs keep banging away at the ominous machine."

At the head of the line is the XO, bellowing, "Come on, Cozzalio, we've got work to do. Get this thing going." Ace is busily turning valves and banging on the pipes. He drips with sweat and stops occasionally to wipe his brow. Eventually, he gives the XO a "thumbs up" and steps away from the steaming apparatus.

Marvin describes what happens next. "The XO walks into the shower, and his towel flops up over the shower wall. We can see his head as he walks up to the spigot, pulls on the chain, and nothing comes out but hot steam, making a loud hissing sound. The XO comes rushing out the shower door. Sounding like a bull, he yells, 'Cozzalio!' We look around and all you can see is Ace running with a cloud of dust behind him as he heads toward the mess hall and continues on to the Officers' Club. The XO is naked, standing in front of the shower, yelling, 'Cozzalio, get your ass back here!' We are all laughing so hard we momentarily forget about hot water."

Ace's first adventure as a plumber is not particularly successful, but within a few days the officers have hot water. Afterward, friends joke with Cozzalio, advising him not to seek a job in plumbing when he gets out of the Army.

Wires Removed

By mid-February, Ace's jaw is healed sufficiently to have the wires removed. It is well past the date the wires would have been removed had he remained in Japan. He has a dilemma—no medical records. He knows that reporting to the hospital to have the wires removed will raise the obvious question: Why doesn't this soldier have medical records?

Ace learns that D Troop is planning a big party at the Officers' Club. Not being one to pass up a party, Cozzalio sees this as an opportunity. He goes to the local hospital, finds a doctor, and demands the wires be removed immediately so he can attend a "troop function."

The doctor explains to Ace that the procedure is very painful, and sedation is necessary.

Ace insists, saying, "Doc, I'm in the cavalry. I can handle it. Take the damn wires out."

Years later he said, "I have never experienced anything so painful in my entire life. And, I was so sick afterwards that I couldn't attend the party."

CLEARED TO FLY

In mid-February, with the wires removed from his jaw, the flight surgeon clears Ace to fly. Initially, he returns to the Longknife Slick Platoon and flies copilot in Hueys. Seeking more excitement, he moves to the Crusader Gun Platoon and flies copilot (gunner) in Charlie Model Huey gunships. Next, the most exciting of all—Warwagons.

CHAPTER 6

WARWAGONS

"If 'Charlie' wants to shoot at a helicopter,
it only costs him his life."

—ACE COZZALIO

IN EARLY APRIL 1968, THE Warwagon Scout Platoon received new
Hughes OH-6A Cayuse helicopters and began transforming its operations to accommodate the new aircraft. The OH-6 was much
different from the OH-23 Raven it replaced. It was considerably
more powerful and maneuverable, enabling a more aggressive
mode of operation.

Ace was assigned to the Scout Platoon on April 10 and, like the
other pilots, needed to learn to operate the new helicopter. He read
the manual and taught himself to fly the OH-6 without formal training. He soon became proficient with the new, highly maneuverable
aircraft and was designated Scout section leader. Weeks later, the
New Equipment Transition Team arrived, providing Ace with formal flight training. Afterward, Ace became the "self-appointed instructor pilot," teaching new Warwagon Scouts to fly the OH-6.

With the arrival of the new aircraft, Ace believed the Scout
Platoon needed a new identity. He thought long and hard about
various names and eventually settled on "Warwagons." He based

this name on the 1967 John Wayne movie of the same title. In the movie, the Warwagon was a heavily armored stagecoach with a Gatling gun mounted on top. This seemed appropriate for the Scouts flying the new OH-6 with "Gatling type" miniguns.

A local Vietnamese sewing shop produced the new Scout Platoon patch with a Warwagon stagecoach overlaying a red and white diagonal background. Soon, all Scout pilots and crew chiefs were wearing the Warwagon patch on their left-side shirt pocket.

WARWAGON PILOTS

Scout pilots were a special breed of helicopter pilot—they had a "wild child" personality and lived for the daily excitement of confronting the enemy with their small helicopter. Most were volunteers, due to the highly dangerous nature of their missions. These pilots were good at their jobs, and they were young enough and cocky enough to think they could fight "Charlie" (VC nickname) face-to-face and always come away the winner.

Scout pilots were less apt to act like officers and instead were often viewed as an audacious bunch of mavericks who flew helicopters. They were a rowdy bunch who lived to the beat of a different drummer—flying consistently hazardous missions in the field and, at times, showing a lack of military discipline on the ground. They fought valiantly and afterward partied heartily. This behavior was tolerated because the Scout pilots risked their lives, day in and day out, and it was difficult to get new volunteers with the proper mind-set and attitude for this treacherous job.

Scout pilots depended on several factors to get through a firefight. In addition to their flying prowess, they were dependent on their crew chief's ability to lay down suppressing fire and their wingman's ability to cover them. Yet, there was one factor the Scouts favored above all others—the minigun. This rotating barrel machine gun was a terrifying weapon. It gave the pilots a significant psychological confidence, creating the impression that, while they were firing it, they were invincible. The minigun made a magnificent loud *BRRRRRRRRRRRRRRRRIP* sound and spit out an awesome flame about two to three feet past the end of the muzzle. In the pilot's mind, and oftentimes reality, the NVA or Vietcong were too busy diving for cover to return fire.[7]

OH-6 Loach Firing the Minigun
Courtesy of U.S. Army Aviation Museum via Ray Wilhite

For Scout pilots, flying the OH-6 and going out to fight Charlie face-to-face was something that could really get your adrenaline going. The Warwagon Scouts fed off of this high, a high that some joked was the next best thing to sex.

THE LOACH

The official Army designation for the OH-6A Cayuse was Light Observation Helicopter (LOH). It wasn't long before it was affectionately nicknamed "Loach." This small, four-bladed helicopter could carry a pilot and four passengers, yet was configured for combat with a crew of two. The Loach provided a quick, highly responsive ride, perfectly suited to the Scout mission of flying low and snooping around.

Hugh Mills, in his book *Low Level Hell*, provides the best description of the Loach:

> The OH-6 had a personality all her own. She was light, nimble, and extremely responsive to every control input. While the Huey was stable, dependable, kind of like the faithful family sedan, the OH-6 was like getting a brand-new MGA Roadster. She was sexy!
>
> The ship was unusually quiet in flight, giving her the added advantage of being practically on top of a potential enemy before anyone on the ground even knew a helicopter was around.
>
> By design, the OH-6 was small and cramped. Her mission gross weight was just over 2,160 pounds. With the main rotor extended, she was only 30 feet, 3 3/4 inches long, and at the pilot's cabin just a fraction over 4 1/2 feet wide. Not much space for [a pilot and crew chief seated] side by side, with an instrument console between them.[8]

There was one characteristic that distinguished the Loach from all other helicopters. The OH-6 was a tough little aircraft. It could absorb an extensive amount of small arms fire and still bring its crew home safely. The Loach was also very crashworthy; its uniquely designed egg-shaped fuselage was wrapped around an A-frame construction that remained intact in a crash, rolling and protecting the crew inside. Many stories exist of crewmembers surviving catastrophic crashes with minimal injuries.

XM-134 7.62 mm Minigun with cowling removed
Courtesy of U.S. Army Aviation Museum via Ray Wilhite

Warwagon Loaches were fitted with the XM-134 six-barrel, 7.62-millimeter minigun, capable of firing two thousand or four thousand rounds per minute. The minigun was mounted on the left side of the Loach, just below the cargo doorsill. The pilot, flying from the right seat (as viewed from inside the aircraft), operated the minigun with a two-position trigger conveniently located on the cyclic control between his legs. Lifting the trigger guard and depressing the trigger to the first detent resulted in a blast of two thousand rounds per minute, while pulling the trigger all the way to the stop brought the massive force of four thousand rounds per minute.

Using grease pencil marks on the windshield as sights, Ace and other Scout pilots aimed their aircraft to hit the target with uncanny precision. The basic load for a mission was two thousand rounds carried in the large ammo can positioned behind the pilot seats in the passenger compartment.

CREW CHIEF/GUNNER

Warwagon crew chiefs (also called gunners or observers) came from various Army duty assignments. Some had been trained as crew chiefs, some had been Huey door gunners, and others were volunteers from the Doughboy Aero-Rifle Platoon. A number of them were combat-hardened infantrymen serving extended tours in Vietnam who volunteered to join Lighthorse and fly Scouts. They had one thing in common: they sought the adventure and excitement that could only come from flying low level in the small, maneuverable OH-6. And, not unlike the Scout pilots, these bold and courageous troopers lived for the daily thrill of confronting the enemy in a face-to-face shootout.

The crew chief, sitting sideways in the left seat of the cockpit, fired a handheld M-60 machine gun supported by a bungee cord attached to the top of the helicopter's doorframe. This configuration gave the gunner an excellent field of fire, covering the entire left flank of the aircraft. The gunner had to be a good marksman with the M-60 as he needed to hit both stationary and moving targets from a helicopter flying thirty to sixty knots (thirty-five to sixty-nine mph) airspeed. He also needed sharp eyesight and the ability to identify evidence of enemy activity (footprints, trash, weapons, hidden bunkers, etc.) from a distance of fifty to a hundred feet as the aircraft sped across the landscape.

In addition to being a good marksman, the gunner also needed to have nerves of steel. While flying in the search mode, the gunner spent a good portion of his time hanging outside the Loach. He would extend his seat belt and shoulder straps as far as possible in order to lean out to look under the aircraft as well as to the front and back. And, he needed a strong constitution to withstand flying at rapid speeds close to the ground while making abrupt changes in speed, altitude, and direction.

Loach Gunner position with Frag Bag
Smoke and CS grenades hanging on wire
Note curved "temporary cyclic stick"
Courtesy of Mike Galvin

The crew chief was also responsible for tossing grenades, effective in knocking out enemy bunkers, hooches, and other structures. Several wires strung along the windshield in front of the gunner held an assortment of incendiary, smoke, CS (tear gas), and Thermite grenades, ready to be dropped on targets. Positioned on the floor between the gunner's feet was a "frag bag." This older type helmet bag or field pack typically contained twenty to twenty-five fragmentation, white phosphorus, and concussion grenades.

MUTUAL TRUST

The bond of trust between the Scout pilot and his crew chief was paramount. They worked together as cohesive partners. The crew chief depended on the pilot's flying skills, and the pilot depended on the crew chief's sharp eyes and M-60 shooting skills. Together they were a team that, after flying together, instinctively knew how the other would react in a firefight.

LOACH MODIFICATIONS

The Warwagons made several modifications to the Loach. To accommodate the gunner firing the M-60 machine gun from the left seat, they installed a flexible ammo chute from a Charlie Model Huey gunship. This chute was attached to a 1,500-round ammo can securely fastened in a welded frame mounted high in the passenger compartment. The chute ran over the gunner's left shoulder, feeding into the left side of the M-60 machine gun. This chute minimized jams and gave the gunner a constant supply of 7.62-millimeter ammo.

Early on, the Warwagons discovered that the cyclic control between the gunner's legs became an obstacle when firing the M-60 machine gun. Maintenance removed the cyclic control tube, leaving an open socket below the gunner's seat cushion. This enabled the gunner to sit sideways in his seat and swing his machine gun in all directions without hitting the controls. Serving as a "temporary cyclic stick," crew chiefs carried a twelve-inch piece of mop handle that inserted in the open cyclic socket, enabling them to fly from the left seat. Warwagon pilots taught their crew chiefs to fly in case the pilot was incapacitated or in those instances when the pilot needed a break. Most gunners personalized their temporary cyclic sticks with designs or notches, and one crew chief used his stick to rap on his pilot's helmet when he needed to get his attention.

SCOUT TACTICS

True to their "Bastard Cav" image, the Warwagon Scouts were unique and their tactics differed from scouts in most other cavalry units. Instead of positioning the crew chief/gunner in the rear seat or having two door gunners, the Warwagons put the single gunner in the front left seat, next to the pilot. Hence, they designed their maneuvers around left-hand turns, giving the gunner maximum visibility and field of fire.

Another distinction was the role of the two Scouts: the lead Scout's job was to seek, engage, and destroy the enemy while the trail Scout's responsibility was to cover and protect the lead aircraft. Working as a cohesive and interdependent team, the two Scouts flew low and slow, nosing into every nook and cranny as they pursued the elusive Vietcong and NVA.

LEAD SCOUT

Always searching, the lead Scout's head was continually "on a swivel" and his eyes were always looking for signs of the enemy's presence—fresh trails, litter, disturbed foliage, campfire ashes, clothing, or equipment. The lead Scout flew so low that he could follow a trail of footprints left by the enemy.

Hovering frequently, he used the helicopter's rotor wash to blow foliage in search of camouflaged fighting positions or enemy soldiers hiding in tall grass. Other times, he hovered to closely inspect a hooch, check out a sampan, or peer deep into tree lines. Upon finding bunkers or spider holes, the lead Scout would aggressively attack using the minigun or grenades. In this slow-moving mode, his objective was to find and aggressively kill the enemy before they had time to react.

A secondary, more perilous motive was to draw hostile fire. Oftentimes, the lead Scout would "recon by fire," a tactic of shooting into a suspicious area in hopes the enemy would return fire and reveal his location. In those instances where the enemy was foolish enough to fire upon the Loaches, the Scouts reacted immediately by returning a barrage of fire from the side-mounted minigun and the gunner's M-60 machine gun. If the situation was overpowering, they called "taking fire" to their Cobra protectors, marked the target with a smoke grenade, and quickly departed, letting the Gunships unleash their heavy firepower.

TRAIL SCOUT

In the search mode, the team of two Loaches flew three to five feet above the ground and obstacles, maintaining ten to twenty-five knots (twenty-nine mph) airspeed. The trail Scout flew off the lead Scout's right side, continually altering his position yet always staying behind the lead aircraft. It was his job to cover lead's unprotected right flank, always ready to engage if the lead aircraft received hostile fire.

Upon finding evidence of enemy activity, the lead Scout slowed to carefully investigate, hovering to take a closer look. When this occurred, the trail Scout would immediately break right and enter a high (fifty- to hundred-feet AGL) left-hand circle around the lead Scout, with his crew chief/gunner constantly covering the lead aircraft with his M-60 machine gun.

While a left-hand orbit provided the tactical firepower advantage with the crew chief covering the left side, it also served as a safety factor. Turning to the left required a little more power to counteract the torque of the main rotor, but it minimized the possibility of encountering "Hughes tailspin." The dreaded tailspin occurred during right-hand decelerating turns at low speed, resulting in loss of tail rotor effectiveness. When this happened the helicopter turned to the right, spinning out of control. Not a good thing when flying close to the ground.

The trail Loach's sole function was to cover the lead Loach. If lead called "taking fire," trail would immediately roll in with minigun and M-60 machine gun blazing. Then the team would reassess and re-engage if necessary. If overwhelmed by a larger force, the two aircraft broke off, letting the Cobra gunships assume the battle.

WARWAGON OFFENSE

Warwagon Scout pilots were taught to take the offensive when fired upon. Ace told new pilots, "If anyone shoots at you, immediately shoot back, putting them on the defensive and swinging the advantage in your favor." Warrant Officer David Newkirk told of Cozzalio flying low level about fifteen to twenty knots (seventeen to twenty-three mph) when he received enemy fire from his right side, the unarmed side of the Loach. "Ace immediately did a pedal turn to the right and laid down a barrage of minigun fire," Newkirk said. "The first time he did that I freaked, because, as his wingman, I had to cover him, doing the same thing. Eventually, I learned to do it. It helped to have the minigun blasting, taking some of the fear out of it."

"CALL US THE BAIT"

In July 1968, Ace was interviewed for *Octofoil,* the 9th Infantry Division magazine. "I guess you could call us the bait," Ace was quoted as saying. "We fly low in hopes the enemy will open fire on us, thereby giving his exact position away. Of course, it would be nice if we saw him first." He added, "Our job is to find and fix the enemy and start the battle. Once we have done this, we move out and let the larger units, who are capable of destroying the enemy, move in."

Ace displayed great confidence in his crew chief. "When the Warwagons open up," he said in the *Octofoil* article, "I'd hate to be underneath them. The mounted miniguns provide area fire, whereas my door gunner could knock the radiator cap off a jeep at 1,000 feet away with his M-60."[9]

ACE'S SCOUTING TRAITS

In addition to his flying skills, Ace possessed a unique trait that made him an exceptional Scout pilot. He had a profound determination to succeed at whatever task he was presented. And, when faced with a developing situation, he was a dynamic thinker, quick to react and forge his own course of action. Once he set his mind on an objective, like finding the Vietcong, he was relentless in his pursuit of the enemy. And, Ace thrived on the thrill and excitement of battle. He was first to volunteer for dangerous missions and, in the spirit of a true cavalryman, was first to fight, no matter where it was.

Ace Flying Warwagon Loach
Wingman at 3 O'clock
Photo by Charles C. Ashton III,
Octofoil magazine

CHAPTER 7

ACE THE SCOUT

"Successful people know how to ride a
horse in the direction it is going."

—ACE COZZALIO

SCOUTS WERE NOT ONLY GOOD pilots, they typically had fast reflexes
and possessed the guts to do what was required with their helicopter. They flew by the "seat of their pants" with their full attention focused outside the aircraft, continuously scanning the area
around them. The Scout pilot was constantly looking out at the
tree line, peering down through the chin bubble, or sticking his
head outside to look directly beneath the aircraft, always looking
for signs of enemy activity.

The key to a Scout's success, and ultimately his survival, was
his awareness of his surroundings. This is where Ace excelled. He
seemed to have an innate ability to detect danger and sense when
the enemy was nearby. He was very perceptive. Trusting his intuition, he often sought out and found the Vietcong and NVA in the
most unexpected locations.

Ace was also a good tracker. Using the skills his grandfather
taught him as a small boy, he could read the bent grass of a trail

and upon finding footprints he could determine how many were in the party, what direction they traveled, and whether they carried heavy loads. Ace aptly described it when he said, "It's just like the old horse cavalry days when the scouts went out to look for the Indians. We go out and look for trails, fresh footprints, campfires, and hidden bunkers. We find 'Charlie' and we are pretty good at it."

SEARCH AND DESTROY – BEN TRE

It is early morning in mid-June 1968. The skies are clear and the wind is calm—a perfect day for flying and a perfect day for hunting the elusive Vietcong. Ace and his wingman, Warrant Officer Bob Grove (Warwagon 15), both flying OH-6 Loaches, are en route to their operations area (AO). They fly low, skirting across the tree-tops at thirty to forty feet altitude and approximately eighty knots (ninety-two mph) airspeed.

Today's assignment is a search and destroy mission—Lighthorse's "bread and butter" mode of operation. The objective is to seek out and attack the enemy, eliminating its forces and destroying its weapons and equipment. The AO for today's mission encompasses a ten-kilometer square area approximately twelve klicks (military slang for kilometers; twelve klicks equals seven miles) southeast of Ben Tre—an area known for heavy Vietcong activity.

This aggressive mission consists of two Warwagon Scouts (Loaches) paired with two newly acquired AH-1G Crusader Gunships (Cobras). Flying low and slow, the Scouts fly at ground level, searching for the enemy. Meanwhile, the Gunships fly at six hundred to eight hundred feet AGL (above ground level) in a race-track (oval) pattern—on call in case the Scouts need firepower from above.

Lighthorse Cav Team
Two Loaches and Two Cobras
Courtesy of Mike Galvin

COMMAND & CONTROL, OR "C&C"

Higher above, flying at one thousand feet altitude in a Huey helicopter, Captain William Whitworth (D Troop's executive officer) is today's air mission commander (AMC). With a tactical map in hand, Whitworth observes the two Loaches below and occasionally calls Cozzalio, giving course corrections along the route.

The Huey and its occupants are called "C&C," meaning Command & Control. The AMC occupies the copilot seat, monitoring the mission from the air and using the aircraft's radios to direct Lighthorse air assets. Most often, the D Troop commanding officer performs the air mission commander role. Other times, like today, the executive officer or senior Lighthorse officers serve as AMC.

VC IN THE STREAM

When the two Loaches are within three klicks (two miles) of the operations area, they come upon a large rice paddy. In tandem, they drop low as they skim across the field of bright green rice plants intersected by long earthen dikes. Approaching the far end of the paddy, they lift up and over the nipa palm trees that border a stream running perpendicular to their course. In a fleeting instant, Ace detects movement in his peripheral vision off his right side, along the stream. He swings his aircraft to the left and calls on the radio, "I got something along this stream. I'm going back to check it out."

"Roger that," replies Whitworth as the C&C Huey starts a slow left-hand orbit high above the Loaches.

The two Scouts make a wide decelerating turn to the left. As they approach the stream, Cozzalio sees ripples spanning out from the bank in the otherwise calm water. It is apparent that some person or large animal jumped into the stream. Ace is suspicious. The Vietcong are known to hide in the water, using reeds to breathe. After a couple of passes along the forty-foot-wide stream, Cozzalio and Grove fly down the stream firing their miniguns into the water near the left bank while their crew chiefs fire their M-60 machine guns into the brush along the bank. Unable to stir up anything, they break off the stream and resume their flight to the operations area.

As they fly along, Ace makes a mental note of the location. His intuition tells him the Vietcong are hiding in the woods near the stream. And, he surmises that the VC will relocate after the Loaches depart. In a tactical ploy, he plans to vacate the area, allowing the enemy time to maneuver. Then he will return and track their movement, anticipating they will leave a trail to their home base.

Arriving at their mission area, the two Scouts start working the tree lines bordering another large rice paddy. After twenty to thirty minutes of finding nothing of significance, Ace calls the air mission commander, saying, "Five, we are heading back to the stream we worked earlier."

Whitworth replies, "Affirmative. I will call for clearance." Then he places a radio call to Battalion Headquarters. Whitworth requests approval to relocate the mission to a new area and submits the map grid coordinates. Minutes later, Battalion returns the call and approves the request.

Arriving at the stream, Ace slows to search the woods near the stream where he saw the disturbance in the water. His wingman, Grove, breaks to the right and enters a wide left-hand circle at about fifty feet altitude. Grove's crew chief aims his M-60 machine gun out the left-side open door frame, ready to shoot if Ace receives hostile fire.

Finding nothing along the stream, Cozzalio lifts his aircraft up and over the dense wooded area and continues his search on the rice paddy side of the woods. Slowly searching along the perimeter of the tree line, he looks carefully for signs of enemy activity. Minutes later, he comes upon a dike running across the rice paddy. There they are—footprints. Ace sets his Loach down with the skids resting crosswise atop the dike. He leans out the right-side open door to take a closer look at the impressions in the dirt.

He calls, "We got a trail. Three sets of tracks."

Whitworth replies, "Copy that. You have clearance to continue and engage if necessary."

Cozzalio brings his Loach to a three-foot hover and follows the tracks as they continue along the dike about four hundred meters (quarter mile) across the rice paddy. On the opposite side, the tracks continue on a well-used path through a grove of nipa palms. Again, Ace lifts his Loach up and over the trees and continues his tracking on the other side. After a few passes along the tree line, he picks up the trail and follows it approximately eight hundred meters (half mile) across a large, open area with low grass and shrubs. There, the trail disappears into dense woods of nipa palm and undergrowth.

VIETCONG BASE CAMP

Once again, Ace lifts his Loach up and over the trees, continuing in the general direction of the path. When his aircraft clears the treetops, he sees his objective—a Vietcong base camp. Ahead, in a clearing approximately 150 meters in the distance, he sees a Vietcong flag atop a fifteen-foot flagpole. In the perimeter of the open area, two small hooches are set back, underneath the fronds of several tall nipa palms.

Surprised by the two helicopters that suddenly emerge over the treetops, a group of twelve to fifteen Vietcong soldiers quickly disperse in multiple directions. Some scramble to grab their weapons while others run and disappear in the dense woods about fifteen meters behind the hooches.

Ace calls, "I've got Victor Charlie in the open. We're going in."

Simultaneously, Cozzalio lifts the collective pitch control and pushes the cyclic forward. The Loach lifts its tail and accelerates across the treetops. Likewise, Grove joins him in the right-side trail position as the two helicopters race toward the encampment.

Two of the VC soldiers reach for weapons and take cover along the side of the hooches while three others grab AK-47s (Soviet 7.62-millimeter rifle with thirty-round curved magazine) and turn to fire upon the rapidly approaching helicopters. About the same time, Cozzalio and Grove have closed to within a hundred meters of the hooches. They open fire with their miniguns, making a loud *BRRRRRRRRRRRRRRRRIP* sound while their crew chiefs hang out the left side of the aircraft firing their M-60 machine guns. *Rat-tat-tat-tat-tat-tat-tat-tat-tat.*

Using the aircraft's pedals, Ace swings the minigun fire left and right. Two of the VC firing at them are hit with the full blast from the minigun ripping through their midsections. In an explosion of blood and body parts, they are blown backward into the grass. The third man turns and runs for cover. Ace's crew chief cuts him down with the M-60 machine gun just before he reaches the tree line. They continue firing as they dive into the camp. At the last moment, they climb up and over the trees.

Banking left, they return to make another pass in front of the camp while the two crew chiefs hang out the left doors of their aircrafts firing M-60 machine guns into and around the hooches. *Rat-tat-tat-tat-tat-tat-tat-tat-tat.* Two VC soldiers carrying rifles emerge from behind the hooches and run for the tree line. The gunners, firing their M-60s, mow them down before they reach the woods.

When it appears the remaining Vietcong have scattered, Cozzalio calls Grove, saying, "One-Five, cover me while I get the flag."

Grove, who thinks it is too risky, replies, "Don't do it, One-Zero. Don't do it."

Ace, determined to get the flag, responds with emphasis. "Cover me," he says as he flies toward the flagpole.

Grove immediately breaks right and lifts upward, entering a left-hand circle while flying around the perimeter of the base camp, covering Cozzalio from an altitude of seventy-five feet.

As he approaches the Vietcong flag, Ace fires a minigun volley near the base of the flagpole. Then he makes a tight circle around the pole looking for trip wires or anything suspicious. Stories of booby-trapped flags give good reason to be cautious. After a close inspection, Cozzalio hovers high above the flagpole. With his left hand, his crew chief holds a fragmentation grenade out the left side door. When directly over the pole, he pulls the pin with his right hand and drops the grenade. As Ace rapidly maneuvers his aircraft away from the flagpole, he hears the *KABOOM* of the grenade and feels the concussion jolt the helicopter.

Circling back, Ace brings his Loach to a high hover alongside the flagpole. Aligning the aircraft's right skid next to the pole, he slides right, pushing the flagpole toward the ground. The pole snaps off about a foot from the base and falls to the earth.

Ace lands his Loach next to the broken flagpole. His crew chief sets his M-60 aside, unbuckles his safety harness, and scrambles to retrieve the flag. As soon as the crew chief is back onboard, Cozzalio lifts off, climbing out of the base camp. Leveling off at seventy-five feet, Grove joins him on the right side and the two Warwagon Scouts depart with their prize.

Once they are clear of the camp, Cozzalio calls, "We've got the flag. Crusader Three-Six, it's your turn."

Crusader 36 replies, "Roger that. Rolling in." He enters a steep dive to commence his attack. The two Cobra Gunships make repeated gun runs, firing rockets, 7.62-millimeter minigun, and forty-millimeter grenades into the woods around the encampment.

After expending their rockets, the Crusader Gunships return to altitude. The Cav Team of five helicopters departs in a northeasterly direction, flying to Ben Tre Airfield to rearm and refuel.

Upon their departure, Whitworth calls Battalion Headquarters and reports the map grid coordinates of the VC base camp. Battalion, in turn, coordinates U.S. Army artillery and Air Force airstrikes that hit the area and effectively destroy what remains of the enemy base camp.[i]

---

i Mission information from Ace Cozzalio's personal audiotape recorded on June 29, 1968

**Ace Cozzalio and Captain William Whitworth
holding captured Viet Cong flag**
Courtesy of Rex Cozzalio

ACE'S HOOCH

Late that evening, the Cav Team returns to Camp Bearcat Airfield. After shutting down and securing their aircraft, the pilots head to the Officer Quarters, a two-story wooden barracks. Ace goes to his room on the first floor, opens the door, and enters. The room has two army cots, a table, and a small refrigerator. In the corner is a set of drums that Ace acquired in Vietnam.

After setting his flight helmet bag on the table, he removes his pistol belt and survival vest, setting them aside. Then he unzips the helmet bag and pulls out the captured VC flag. The flag's fabric is faded and the edges are tattered, indications that today's enemy was a hardcore Vietcong unit, in existence for a long time.

Hanging on the wall near Ace's cot is a large eagle sculpture, a gift to Ace from his mother, Jan. He drapes one end of the VC flag through the eagle's beak and the other end through the extended claw, making it appear as if the eagle is ripping the flag apart. Then Ace stands back and admires his creation, thinking, "We kicked ass today. We found the Vietcong and destroyed them."

OTHER WARWAGON MISSIONS

While the primary mode of operation for the Warwagons is the search and destroy mission with the Scouts down low, seeking the enemy's location, they also perform other functions for the cavalry troop. They scout and mark the landing zones for Longknife Lift Platoon troop insertions. On occasion, they extract and medevac downed aircrew. And, the Scouts fly cover for the slow-moving "sniffer" Huey. In this role, they follow closely behind the Huey, ready to return fire and protect the larger helicopter should enemy forces attempt to engage it.

CHAPTER 8

SHOT DOWN ON
SNIFFER MISSION

ONE OF THE NEW TECHNOLOGIES used in the Vietnam War was the
"people sniffer." The sniffer was a Huey helicopter rigged with special equipment that detected the presence of human activity. This
Huey had two large air scoops, one attached to the front of each
skid. Long tubes ran from the scoops, through the open cargo
door, and into a special console strapped to the passenger compartment floor behind the aircraft radios. A sniffer operator sat
behind the console peering into a visor-covered screen. He called
out "mark" or "hot" to the pilots when the sniffer sensed human
activity, and the copilot marked the location on the map. A concentration of "hot" readings in a particular area would result in
airstrikes or combat assaults to rout out the enemy.

The sniffer worked on the premise that the human body
gives off ammonia when sweating; the equipment was so sensitive that it could detect the presence of ammonia in the air
currents. To accurately detect human activity, the sniffer Huey
flew low and slow, in a crosshatch pattern while taking readings.
This mode of flying made the slow-moving helicopter a "sitting
duck" target for enemy small arms fire. To deal with this threat,
the sniffer Huey door gunners were on constant alert with M-60

machine guns ready and eyeballs straining for that enemy soldier who might jump out of the tree line and fire his AK-47 at the slow-moving aircraft.[10]

For Lighthorse sniffer missions, two Cobra Gunships escorted the sniffer-equipped Huey. Since the Cobras were ineffective when flying at lower airspeeds, they flew high above the sniffer, on guard to dive with rockets and minigun fire should the slow-moving Huey take fire. To provide a more immediate response, a team of two OH-6 Loaches flew directly behind the sniffer Huey.

LONGKNIFE SNIFFER MISSION— PLAIN OF REEDS

It is July 1968 and D Troop is flying a sniffer mission in the Plain of Reeds, about thirty klicks (nineteen miles) west of Tan An. The Plain of Reeds is an enormous marshy area, stretching from Tan An in the east to the Cambodian border in the northwest, a distance of about 110 kilometers (sixty-eight miles), and is sixty kilometers (thirty-seven miles) at its widest. Its name is derived from the vast open areas of tall reeds and elephant grass growing out of waist-deep, leech-infested water. Infantry soldiers call this area the "Sea of Reeds"; when looking down from aircraft, the grasses look like waves as they undulate in the wind.

During the monsoon season (May–September), this vast area floods as the level of the Mekong River rises. In the dry season (October–April), water from the canals and streams flows back into the Upper Mekong River, pulling water out of the Plain. As a result, some areas are covered in water for the entire year. Others contain swamps hundreds of meters long where water is knee-deep with thick mud, and yet in other areas the soil is dry and parched.[11]

Widely recognized as a sanctuary for the Vietcong, the Plain of Reeds with its wood-lined canals and thick vegetation gives

"Charlie" plenty of places to hide. Accordingly, this area is ideal for the people sniffer since it can effectively detect the presence of humans hiding in tall reeds and grasses as well as the dense vegetation along the canals.

THE MISSION

First Lieutenant David Conrad is aircraft commander flying a Longknife Huey outfitted with the sniffer equipment. A team of two Warwagon Loaches, with Ace Cozzalio in the lead, trails the sniffer Huey as it flies low and slow, crisscrossing the wide plains. Two Crusader Cobra Gunships fly above at seven hundred feet AGL, on call to provide heavy fire support if needed. The C&C Huey flies higher at one thousand feet AGL. Onboard the C&C Huey, Major Duane Brofer, D Troop Commanding Officer, serves as today's air mission commander, carefully observing the sniffer Huey and two Loaches below.

It is 1600 hours as the sniffer Huey team flies a straight path across several kilometers of tall reeds and grasses. Passing over a wood line at the far end, the Huey makes a wide 180-degree turn to the left and lines up to fly another course. This pattern repeats time after time as they continue their crosshatch pattern across the large open area.

After about forty minutes, they haven't detected anything with the sniffer equipment, so Brofer instructs the team to relocate to a nearby sector for one last try before returning to Camp Bearcat.

Since the new location is nearby, Conrad decides to fly low level instead of bringing his Huey to altitude. He breaks off his sniffer pattern and turns to the northwest, heading for the new sector. After crossing a long, wide-open area of reeds and grasses, they come upon rice paddies with dikes sectioning the fields into large rectangles. A densely wooded area borders the far side of the paddies.

The three aircraft sweep low across the bright green rice fields. As they approach the far side of the paddies, Conrad swings to the right, heading for a clearing in the wood line. Three or four hooches (Vietnamese dwellings) are located in the edge of the trees on both sides of the clearing.

"It is an unwritten rule for helicopter pilots that you never fly between two hooches," said Conrad. "But that day, I am in a hurry and decide to risk it."

ACE SHOT DOWN

Flying at twenty feet altitude, Conrad's sniffer Huey flies between the hooches without incident. It seems the Vietcong never shoot at the first aircraft—that just alerts them to be ready for the next one, and that is Ace. When his Loach passes between the hooches, the VC open up with AK-47 fire, riddling his aircraft. Neither Ace nor his door gunner is wounded, and it happens so fast that they don't have an opportunity to return fire.

Cozzalio calls on the radio: "We're hit, and I have oil spraying out of the transmission. I'm heading out to the middle of this open area to set down where nobody can get to us." He continues flying while transmission oil sprays into the cockpit. Ace realizes he needs to get the Loach on the ground quickly. If the transmission locks up, the rotors stop turning, and the resulting crash can be deadly.

Hearing Ace's radio call, Conrad immediately swings the cyclic control to the right, making a tight right turn. He circles around to follow the crippled aircraft, closing at about one hundred knots (115 mph) airspeed. Shortly thereafter, the Loach starts tumbling in midair. Apparently a flight control push-pull tube to the rotor head had taken a hit and separated, causing the aircraft to lose control. Conrad sees Ace's Loach tumble at least three times in midair before impacting in the rice paddy.

"I am about fifty yards behind Ace when he loses control and I almost hit him when the helicopter starts to decelerate as it is flipping in the air," said Conrad. "I veer to the right and pull back on the cyclic and lower the collective to slow my airspeed. The crashing Loach sends water spraying in all directions. I'm still going too fast to land nearby. As I pass by Ace, I stand on the left pedal and slip the Huey sideways, doing a backwards flare in a 180-degree turn. Then I wallow into the rice paddy about fifty yards past the crash. The old D Model Huey is straining, and I still don't know how I keep from crashing. Once the Huey settles into the rice paddy, I look over at Ace. He and his gunner are still sitting in the helicopter. The aircraft's tail is sticking in the mud, and the rotor blades are missing. The cockpit is tilted upward; the Plexiglas bubble is gone and Ace is facing me. He looks up and impolitely gives me the 'finger of fate.' He lets me know I am the one who screwed up and got him shot down."

Ace removes his flight helmet, unbuckles his safety harness, and climbs out of the crumpled wreckage. Then he goes to the other side of the aircraft and helps his crew chief crawl out. He and his gunner are relatively unscathed. Walking around the crashed aircraft, Ace finds that his OH-6 is totally destroyed with little to salvage.

In the meantime, Conrad repositioned his Huey to the left side of the crashed Loach. Conrad's crew chief and door gunner quickly remove their helmets, unbuckle their safety harnesses, and exit the aircraft. Then they slog through the calf-deep water of the rice paddy to assist the dazed Loach crew. Together they retrieve the guns, grenades, radios, and aircraft logbook, taking them to Conrad's Huey. After about fifteen minutes, their equipment and weapons are loaded, and Conrad is ready to depart.

In the meantime, the crash has caught the attention of Charlie. Ace's wingman calls Brofer, the air mission commander, reporting a large contingent of Vietcong moving through the woods toward the crash site.

Brofer realizes it is impossible to arrange for sling load to retrieve the crashed aircraft this late in the day. And, to further complicate matters, the Cav Team is low on fuel, and there are no aircraft available to remain on station. Brofer calls Conrad, instructing him to use a thermite grenade to burn what remains of the busted aircraft.

Returning to the crash site, Ace lets his crew chief do the honors. The gunner walks over to the crumpled aircraft, pulls the pin on a thermite grenade, and tosses it into the cargo compartment near the engine. Then Ace and his crew chief scramble to the waiting Huey.

This photo was taken from the C&C Huey flying above the crash site. The Loach impacted upside down with its rotors in the rice paddy and rolled approximately 170 feet. Conrad's Huey is to the left of the burning Loach.

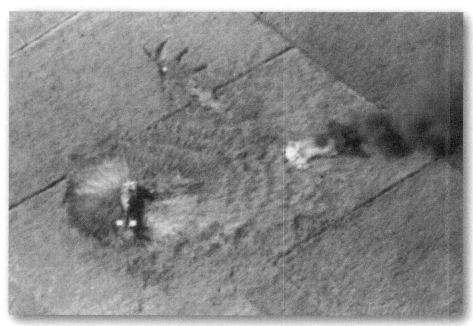

Ace's burning Loach
Courtesy of David Conrad

As Ace climbs aboard the Slick, he turns to Conrad and announces in a loud voice, "Conrad, you are damned sure buying the beer tonight." And, that evening Conrad gladly complies and buys a round of drinks for D Troop.

It is a common occurrence for the pilots to meet at the O-Club to "let off steam," and celebrate after a long day's mission. The camaraderie and esprit de corps in D Troop is extremely high. The pilots and crew fly together as a cohesive team. And, if one of their team is shot down or otherwise in peril, they never hesitate to put their lives on the line for their fellow trooper. Over time, this instills a high level of pride that permeates all they do. For Ace, this "cavalry pride" is paramount, and he continually seeks ways to promote the character and charisma of the 1860s horse cavalry within D Troop.

CHAPTER 9

STETSONS, SCARVES, AND SABERS

*"I was with a super cavalry troop. We did not fight
for God, country, mother, and apple pie—we fought
for our unit and the people in the cavalry."*

—ACE COZZALIO

YELLOW SCARVES

IN AN EFFORT TO DISTINGUISH Lighthorse as a unique cavalry troop, Ace initiates several uniform enhancements. Recalling the western movies he had seen as a boy, he decides yellow scarves would be appropriate for D Troop. Besides, yellow was the branch color for the U.S. Cavalry that later became the Armor Branch in 1950. Ace sends a letter to his mother requesting yellow triangular scarves for the entire troop. His mom, Jan, bought the material, and Ace's grandmother cut and sewed the scarves.

In July 1968 a large box arrives, and soon every D Trooper is wearing a yellow scarf tied loosely around his neck. The Lighthorse Troopers wear their scarves everywhere: in the field, around the base camp, and in the troop area. It seems that some of the troopers are so proud of that scarf that they never take it off. And, Ace doesn't stop there—this is just the beginning.

White Cav Hats

While other cavalry units in Vietnam wear black "Cav hats," Ace believes Lighthorse should be different. He meets with First Lieutenant Frank Bryan and Second Lieutenant Tony Ziemiecki. Together they conspire to acquire white Stetson cavalry hats. This seems a fitting image for D/3-5 Cavalry, since the 5th U.S. Cavalry fought in the late 1800s Indian campaigns. During those days, the white (the official color is "silver belly") hat was the working hat of the horse cavalry while the black hat was worn with the dress uniform. Since Lighthorse is continually in the field, mixing it up with the enemy, the "working hat" seems most appropriate.

When asked, Ace proudly proclaims another reason for the white Stetsons. Lieutenant Colonel Robert E. Lee commanded the 5th Cavalry's predecessor, 2nd Cavalry, until he resigned his commission to join the Confederacy in 1861.[12] As everyone knows, General Lee always wore a white hat.

The three troopers contact the Stetson hat factory in St. Joseph, Missouri, and make arrangements for a special production run of silver belly cavalry hats. Each hat comes adorned with gold (officer) or silver (warrant officer) cords with acorns on each end that fall across the front brim. The hats also have the cavalry black leather chinstraps that, instead of being worn under the chin, are draped across the back of the neck.

Sabers

To further distinguish themselves as a cavalry unit, they decide to acquire regulation officer sabers. They find a supplier of Model 1902 U.S. Army officer sabers. This saber has an engraved blade with an eagle, cannons, and U.S. markings. The blade is dull, shiny, and designed for ceremonial use.

Rallying the D Troop officers together, they take orders for silver belly Stetsons and officer sabers. In late August, the Cav hats and sabers arrive. The troopers attach brass crossed sabers insignia on the front crown of their Cav hats and custom shape the brim to their individual taste.

Soon, Ace and his fellow Lighthorse Troopers are proudly wearing their white hats, yellow scarves, and sabers in sharp contrast to the pilots and crewmembers of other units. It is a common occurrence for new arrivals to see the D Troopers and ask, "Who are those guys?" The usual reply is, "That's the Cav!"

D Troop's identity is firmly established. They are a unique cavalry troop, and their new image serves to further align them as the "Bastard Cav." For Ace, Frank, and Tony, they will initiate even more cavalry uniform enhancements in the days to come.

Ace's Work Saber

In addition to the Model 1902 officers saber, Ace acquires an 1860s Civil War light cavalry saber. This saber has a wide, stout blade and leather-wrapped grip protected by a brass hand guard. Ace has the blade sharpened and carries this saber in his Loach while flying combat missions.

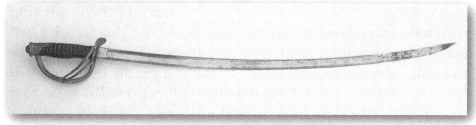

Ace's Civil War Cavalry Saber

Note: Referred to as the M1860 pattern, Ace's Civil War saber was manufactured by Mansfield and Lamb in Forrestdale, Rhode Island. Making 37,458 sabers, the company was the second largest domestic producer of cavalry sabers during the Civil War.[13]

Likely used by a Union cavalry trooper in the Civil War, this hundred-year-old saber is once again carried into battle by a cavalryman. Instead of a horse, this trooper rides in a turbine-powered helicopter. There are many stories about Ace and his saber. Some stretch the imagination, like the story of Ace flying low and fast across the open terrain while swinging his saber out the right side of the Loach as he chases the Vietcong. While that story is a little hard to believe, there are other well-documented stories of Ace using his saber when he dismounts his aircraft, taking prisoners or dealing with a situation on the ground. Undoubtedly, this impressive sword had a huge psychological impact when viewed by the enemy.

THE SABER AND THE BAR BELL

On one occasion, Ace found another use for his saber. Cozzalio and a group of five other Lighthorse pilots, all wearing their yellow scarves, silver belly Stetsons, and sabers, walk into the 9th Division Officers' Club. Approaching the bar, the six troopers order their drinks. About that time, an older lieutenant colonel sitting at the bar looks up at the six troopers boldly standing there, wearing their white Cav hats. The lieutenant colonel, looking as if he had one too many drinks, reaches to his left about four feet and grabs the long, leather cord attached to the clapper in the brass bell hanging above the bar. He rings the bell repeatedly, expecting the cavalry officers to buy a round of drinks. (Military tradition dictates that if you wear your hat into the bar, you are obligated to buy a round of drinks. The bell ringing serves to announce the infraction.)

Initially ignoring the bell, Ace decides to put an end to this nonsense. He walks over to the lieutenant colonel. With his right hand he pulls his Civil War saber from its sheath, and with one slash across the bar he severs the leather cord and it falls limp on the bar top. The O-Club becomes amazingly silent as Ace returns his saber to its sheath and calmly walks back to his buddies on the other side of the bar. There, they continue with their drinks and have a good time—while wearing their Cav hats.

ACE'S REVOLVER

For sidearms, Army pilots are issued either the Colt M1911 .45 caliber automatic pistol or the Smith & Wesson .38-caliber revolver. True to style, Ace carried a Colt .357-caliber western style revolver in a western holster attached to a gun belt with a row of cartridges in shell loops. He wore this low-slung western style holster and revolver on all missions—old west indeed.

"THE OLD CAV" IN THE MEKONG DELTA

Yes, Ace had a romanticized notion of how a cavalry troop should look. Harkening back to the days of the horse cavalry, Ace imagined the troopers wearing dashing uniforms in the setting of an old cavalry stockade. After implementing yellow scarves and silver belly Cav hats, Ace made plans to remake the Lighthorse Troop area in the image of an old 1860s cavalry fort. Laying out plans, he set aside an area to construct a horse stable and had Warrant Officer Gary Winsett build a ten-foot-long watering trough and hitching post in front of D Troop Headquarters. It was then that Ace announced, "What we need is a cavalry horse." Already having an old saddle, he planned to acquire a horse and ride him in the troop area.

One day he approaches Winsett. "Come with me," he says. "We are flying to Saigon to find a horse." Gary grabs his flight gear and follows Ace to the flight line, where they climb into a Loach and take off for Saigon. After landing at Tan San Nhut Airbase, they shut down the aircraft and Ace makes arrangements to "borrow" a jeep. After driving twenty minutes, they come upon an old horse-racing track. After spending several hours looking at a few old swayback horses grazing in fields near the abandoned track, Ace decides that none of the animals meet the high standards of the cavalry. The two return to Saigon and fly back to Dong Tam (D Troop relocated to Dong Tam in October 1968).

On the return trip, Winsett asks, "When you find the right horse, how will you get him to Dong Tam?" Gary almost expects Ace to say he will saddle up and ride the horse to Dong Tam. Instead, he replies, "Oh, I've got that covered. I will put the horse in a Chinook (tandem rotor heavy-lift helicopter) helicopter and tranquilize him. One of the Chinook pilots has agreed to fly him back to Dong Tam."

Ace continued his search for a cavalry horse but never found an adequate steed for D Troop. He did, however, come up with an even more realistic cavalry uniform.

1860s Cavalry Uniform

One day in September, Lighthorse Troopers see an unusual sight emerge from the officer barracks—three cavalry officers (Ace, Frank, and Tony) in complete 1860s cavalry uniforms. Each is wearing their silver belly Stetson with crossed sabers on the front and gold cord around the crown with two acorns falling near the brim. Around their neck, a yellow scarf hangs over an indigo blue blouse with yellow shoulder boards denoting their rank. Their blue trousers with yellow stripes along the side of the legs are tucked into high riding boots with silver spurs. Around their waist is a black leather Sam Browne belt with a shiny cavalry saber hanging from the left side. What a sight! The horse cavalry of the 1860s is resurrected! Thereafter, this uniform is worn at Lighthorse award ceremonies and special occasions. Keep in mind that having a beer with fellow D Troopers is always a special occasion.

Tony Ziemiecki in 1860s Cavalry Uniform
Photo taken in front of Custer's Cafeteria, the troop mess hall
Courtesy of Gary Winsett

PICKING UP NEWBIES

Having a great sense of humor, Ace takes delight in "messing with" new guys arriving in Vietnam. Warrant Officer Mike Rasbury tells of his arrival at Dong Tam as a new pilot. He reports to the 9th Aviation Headquarters and is told he is assigned to the cavalry. The sergeant says, "Take a seat, and someone will come get you."

Rasbury tells what happened next. "The door opens and there stands First Lieutenant Ace Cozzalio. Six-foot-two, skinny as a rail, and standing tall. He is wearing a white Stetson with crossed sabers on the front. A yellow scarf around his neck hangs loose on an 1860s cavalry shirt, dark blue with gold buttons and shoulder boards. Dress blue pants are tucked into riding boots with silver spurs. Around his waist is a saber on the left and pistol on the right. On his chest hangs a Silver Star and Purple Heart. His neck is bandaged and still bleeding. In a commanding voice that demands immediate respect, he said, 'I'm here for my men.' My whole life flashes before my eyes. I didn't know it then, but the rest of my life will be profoundly affected by the man in the door."

Another pilot, First Lieutenant Les Smith, tells a similar story of Ace picking him up in the 1860s cavalry uniform. Ace strides through the door and calls out in a loud voice, "Grab your gear and follow me." They go outside, and Ace tells Smith to throw his gear in the back of a nasty old ¾-ton truck with "Loach Coach" painted on the hood.

Ace climbs behind the wheel and drives to the troop area with Smith wondering, "What have I gotten myself into? Is this guy for real or crazy? Is the whole troop crazy? Turns out we were all crazy, just to varying degrees."

CHAPTER 10

COBRA COVER

CAI LAY—AUGUST 2, 1968

IN THE EARLY AFTERNOON, THREE Huey helicopters from the Longknife
Slick Platoon fly in trail formation (one aircraft behind the other)
at 1,200 feet altitude, high above the marshy wetlands northwest of
Cai Lay, in the Plain of Reeds. Flying in a westerly direction, they
carry eighteen troopers from the Doughboy Aero-Rifle Platoon to
be inserted in an area several klicks ahead.

DOUGHBOYS

The Doughboy Aero-Rifle Platoon was employed as a light infantry strike force. After being inserted by the Longknife Slicks, the
Aero-Rifle Platoon conducted reconnaissance, ambushes, battle
damage assessments, and aircraft rescue or recovery.

Commanded by a platoon leader and platoon sergeant, the
Doughboys were comprised of four six-man fire teams. Each team
was equipped with five M-16 rifles, an M-79 grenade launcher, and
a PRC-25 radio. Functioning primarily as a quick-reaction team,
they focused on remaining light and nimble, averting the extra
weight of the M-60 machine gun and other arms that would slow
their movement.

Depending on the situation, two or three fire teams of Dough-boys, led by the platoon leader or platoon sergeant, were inserted in an operation area to perform their assigned mission. In today's mission, three fire teams are being inserted to perform a battle damage assessment.

CAV TEAM *LZ* RECON

Flying alongside the three Slicks is the C&C Huey with Major Duane Brofer in the copilot's seat, functioning as the air mission commander for today's mission.

Meanwhile, two Warwagon Scouts with Ace Cozzalio in the lead aircraft are performing a VR (visual reconnaissance) of the landing zone (LZ). Flying low and slow, the two Scouts make a thorough recon of the open area looking for booby traps, bunkers, enemy lurking in spider holes, or other hazards. High above, two Crusader Cobras fly a racetrack pattern at six hundred feet covering the two Loaches as they make their inspection. In time, Cozzalio calls Brofer and reports that the LZ is clear for landing.

Brofer calls on the troop push, "Longknife Two-Six, this is Lighthorse Six. The LZ is at your one o'clock, about five klicks (three miles) ahead. You have suppression inbound." (This radio transmission notifies the Longknife Platoon that they are near the landing zone and cleared to land. Suppression means they have permission to fire their door guns on final approach since the woods bordering the LZ are known to be hostile.)

Longknife 26 replies, "Roger that. Suppression inbound."

Then Brofer makes another radio call. "Warwagon One-Zero, pop a smoke."

After dropping a colored smoke grenade in the far end of the landing zone, Warwagon 10 (Cozzalio) replies, "Smokes out." The two Loaches exit the LZ, flying to the south.

DOUGHBOY INSERTION

After making a slight course correction to the right, Longknife lead sees the smoke directly ahead as it swirls upward from an open area bordered by a densely wooded area on the right flank. Longknife lead calls, "Longknife Two-Six has a tally on purple smoke."

Cozzalio replies, "Purple it is."

Shortly thereafter, Longknife lead calls, "Slicks inbound." He commences his descent at a rate of five hundred feet per minute. Simultaneously, the other Hueys commence their descent, flying in tight trail formation with each aircraft positioned slightly higher than the aircraft ahead of them. This formation is often used for troop insertions because it provides maximum door gunner firepower on both flanks of the three helicopters.

When the Hueys are about two hundred feet above the ground, each aircraft commander announces on the aircraft intercom, "Gunners, go hot," and the door gunners fire their M-60 machine guns—*rat-tat-tat-tat-tat-tat-tat-tat-tat*—as the Slicks continue their approach.

Seconds later, the three Hueys flare nose high to reduce airspeed and settle into the landing zone. Crusader Cobras pound the densely wooded area along their right flank with 2.75-inch rockets, 7.62-millimeter minigun fire, and forty-millimeter grenades. The aircraft commanders announce "cease fire" as the Slicks terminate their approach to a hover. Eighteen Doughboys jump off the helicopter skids into knee-deep water and tall elephant grass, quickly moving away from the helicopters.

Once the doughboys have dismounted, the Longknife aircraft commanders call on the radio, "One's up.... Two's up.... Three's up." Then Longknife lead calls, "Slicks will be coming out at two seven zero." (That means the Hueys will be departing on a compass heading of 270 degrees.)

In unison, the three Hueys nose over with their tails high in the air, gaining airspeed as they make a hasty departure in trail formation. Once clear of the landing zone, the aircraft commanders announce, "Go hot." The door gunners open up on their departure. *Rat-tat-tat-tat-tat-tat-tat-tat-tat.*

Meanwhile, the Cobras continue to blast the dense wooded area on their right flank. After the Slicks climb to above three hundred feet altitude, the aircraft commanders announce, "Cease fire." The door gunners quit firing and return their M-60 machine guns to the ready position.

Flying to a nearby ARVN outpost, the three Longknife pilots shut down their aircraft and maintain a "ready" status, on call to extract the Doughboys.

The two Crusader Cobras and the C&C Huey remain on location, flying orbits above the Doughboys on the ground.

BATTLE DAMAGE ASSESSMENT

The Doughboys promptly form an assault line facing the dense woods 150 yards to their front. In an earlier search and destroy mission, the Lighthorse Cav Team attacked a substantially sized enemy force in the woods. After an extended battle, the enemy was thought to be neutralized. The Doughboys are tasked to sweep through the woods, confirming enemy dead and gathering information about the enemy forces.

As the Doughboys approach the tree line, they see the wooded area is a shambles. Trees are stripped of all vegetation, leaving bare trunks looking like tall telephone poles. Others are blown over, leaning on those remaining. Fires are burning in several locations, and smoke filters throughout the area.

Upon reaching the edge of the woods, they discover three dead Vietcong soldiers dressed in black "pajamas" (black shirt and trousers) and Ho Chi Minh sandals (sandals made from tire treads). They find no weapons, a tip-off that other VC may be alive and lurking in the shadows. Further down the tree line, they find a destroyed bunker with two dead Vietcong inside. Again, no weapons are found.

In the meantime, the trail Cobra, flying a racetrack pattern high above, experiences a mechanical problem and returns to Camp Bearcat, leaving one gunship on location.

On the ground, the Doughboys maneuver carefully through the tangled undergrowth of vegetation. About thirty meters into the woods, a Vietcong soldier jumps up and runs, quickly disappearing in the remaining trees. Instinctively, the Doughboys open fire on the elusive VC, and the woods explode with enemy fire from multiple directions. The Doughboys promptly take cover and return fire.

Realizing they are outnumbered, the Doughboy team leader makes a radio call to the air mission commander (Brofer) requesting air support. Brofer, concerned about air strikes in the proximity of the Doughboys, calls the Warwagon Scouts, instructing them to fly over and mark the enemy location for the Cobra Gunship.

Scouts Out

Ace Cozzalio has been monitoring the radio chatter from an area seven hundred meters to the south. Flying low level, he and his wingman arrive and line up on the west end of the woods. They fly fast, skimming across the treetops, and locate the Doughboys, who are taking cover about thirty meters inside the woods. Upon reaching the east end of the tree line, the Loaches make a sweeping right turn over the open marsh and make their approach perpendicular to the wooded area, flying directly over the D Troopers.

As the Loaches pass over the Doughboys, they immediately take AK-47 fire from the enemy. With miniguns and M-60s blazing, Ace and his wingman fly directly at the Vietcong. Just before they reach the enemy's location, Cozzalio's crew chief drops a red smoke grenade. Ace calls, "Crusader Three-Seven, smoke's out.

Direct your fire north of the smoke." Then the Scouts quickly depart the area.

Seconds later, Crusader 37 calls, "Three-Seven, inbound hot on the red smoke." Flying in a westerly direction, the Cobra commences a gun run, firing rockets and the minigun into the area marked by the smoke. When the Cobra breaks to climb, a multitude of green tracer rounds streak upward from the wooded area. Crusader 37 calls, "Taking fire, taking fire, TAKING HITS." Without a wingman, the Cobra is vulnerable, having no covering fire on his departure.

As the Cobra climbs to altitude, Ace calls, "Crusader Three-Seven, Warwagon One-Zero. I'll cover your next run. Break left after dropping your load, so I don't shoot ya."

Crusader 37 responds, "Roger that, I can use the cover." He circles back and lines up to commence another gun run in a westerly direction. Then he calls, "Crusader Three-Seven is inbound hot."

Ace replies, "Roger that. I'm on your left flank." Flying three hundred feet above the marsh, Ace flies a parallel course to the diving Cobra. When Crusader 37 breaks to climb, Ace, covered by his wingman, turns into the woods and dives directly into the enemy positions with minigun and M-60 blazing. Receiving a barrage of enemy small arms fire, the Plexiglas bubble on his Loach explodes, sending shards of plastic into the cockpit. Undaunted, he continues his attack. At the last moment, he lifts high above the woods and banks to the left, returning to the open marsh.

Ace decides he has enough ammo for one more attack. He and his wingman line up on the woods, flying in an easterly direction. As the two Loaches close on the Vietcong positions, the pilots fire their miniguns while their crew chiefs drop fragmentation grenades on the enemy below. Then they swing to the right, returning to the open area seven hundred meters to the south and land to access their damage. In addition to the busted Plexiglas windscreen, both Loaches have several bullet holes in the fuselage and tail boom.

DOUGHBOYS EXTRACTED

In the midst of the Cobra/Loach battle, the Doughboys withdraw out of the woods and cross the open area about two hundred meters to a pick-up zone in the middle of the marshy wetlands. They call the air mission commander, who, in turn, alerts the Longknife Lift Platoon to extract the Doughboys.

In a matter of minutes, the three Longknife Slicks can be heard in the distance: *Wop, Wop, Wop, Wop, Wop.* The Doughboys toss a yellow smoke grenade into the pick-up zone and call, "Longknife Two-Six, Doughboy Four-Six. Smoke's out."

Longknife 26 replies, "I've got a tally on yellow smoke." Doughboy 46 replies, "Roger, yellow smoke."

The three Slicks line up on final approach as the door gunners ready their M-60 machine guns. Since the landing zone is hot, Longknife lead announces, "Flight, this is Two-Six. We are going in low. You have suppression inbound and outbound." In trail formation, the Hueys drop to about fifty feet AGL and race toward the yellow smoke in the distance. The aircraft commanders announce, "Go hot," and the door gunners fire into the wood line.

Closing on the landing zone, the three Slicks flare nose upward as they slow and come to a hover with the nose of the lead Huey about twenty feet from the swirling yellow smoke. The door gunners continue firing as the Hueys settle low with their skids barely in the water while the Doughboys scramble to climb aboard. Enemy fire from the wood line hits in the water around the three Slicks, and a few plinking sounds can be heard when the bullets rip through the thin aluminum skin of the Hueys.

As before, the three Huey pilots call on the radio, "One's up.... Two's up.... Three's up." Then Longknife lead calls, "Slicks are headed home." In unison, the three Hueys drop their noses and lift their tails as they fly low (fifteen to twenty feet AGL), gaining airspeed while the door gunners fire M-60 machine guns upon their departure. Upon reaching ninety knots (104 mph), the pilots pull back on the cyclic control and do a cyclic climb, rapidly ascending in sequence—one, two, three Slicks upward. At about five hundred feet altitude, the door gunners cease firing. The Doughboys are recovered with no casualties.

Once the Longknife Hueys reach 1,500 feet altitude, they are joined by the single Crusader Cobra and the C&C Huey. Together, the Cav Team turns to the east heading for Tan An to refuel before the return flight to Camp Bearcat. The two Loaches fly below at five hundred feet altitude. For Ace, the wind whistling through the shattered windscreen makes the return trip breezy, not unlike the open cockpit aircraft of yesteryear.

For his outstanding flying ability and devotion to duty, Ace Cozzalio is awarded the Distinguished Flying Cross (DFC). This is one of four DFCs that Ace received during his Vietnam tour.

CHAPTER 11

SNIFFER PILOT RESCUE

DINH TUONG PROVINCE—AUGUST 19, 1968

IN THE DAWN OF EARLY morning, a Cav Team of six helicopters departs Camp Bearcat Airfield heading in a southerly direction. On
today's mission, Ace Cozzalio is flying lead Scout to provide cover
for a people sniffer Huey. His crew chief, Specialist 4 William "Wilt"
Chamberlain (all five-foot-four of him), accompanies Cozzalio in
the left seat of the Loach. Ace and Wilt have flown together on many
missions. Together, they are a remarkable Scout team, anticipating
each other's actions and reactions in an uncanny way. Little do they
realize that they are soon to be challenged in an unexpected and
highly dangerous situation—a rescue from a burning aircraft.

The sniffer Huey aircraft commander is Warrant Officer Ken
Lake. Lake has been in-country four months and is an experienced Huey pilot. He has flown this mission previously and is
well acquainted with the sniffer operation. His copilot, Warrant
Officer Brock McCloskey, has been in-country two months and is
also an experienced pilot. Onboard Lake's aircraft are his crew
chief, door gunner, and two sniffer operators manning the sniffer
equipment in the cargo compartment.

The air mission commander for today's mission is Major Duane
Brofer. Accompanying Brofer as aircraft commander of the C&C
Huey is First Lieutenant Marvin Fuller.

Escorted by two Crusader Cobra Gunships, the Cav Team of six helicopters departs Camp Bearcat. They are flying south to refuel at Dong Tam Airfield before continuing today's mission in the Plain of Reeds.

WAGON WHEEL

After refueling, Brofer and Fuller, in the C&C Huey, venture ahead of the group to perform an aerial reconnaissance of the operations area. The remaining five helicopters reposition from the refueling pads and shut down alongside the Dong Tam runway, waiting the call to launch for today's mission.

After twenty to thirty minutes, Brofer makes a call on the troop push. "Troop, this is six. Mount up and head out. We will meet you en route to the AO."

Hearing Brofer's radio call, one of the pilots hollers, "Let's go," and the crewmembers scramble to their aircraft. Soon, the sound of turbine engines fills the air and rotor blades start to turn. In less than two minutes, the five aircraft are ready for takeoff.

After bringing his OH-6 to operating rpm, Cozzalio looks to his wingman positioned on his right side. The wingman gives a "thumbs up" signal and Ace calls, "Scouts are up."

Seconds later, Crusader 36 calls, "Guns are up."

Lake calls the airfield tower for takeoff clearance. "Dong Tam Tower, this is Longknife Two-Eight with a flight of five, requesting clearance for departure to the west."

The tower responds, giving departure clearance for runway 280. Then the pilots of the five helicopters bring their aircraft to a three-feet hover and move to the center of the tarmac. They do a pedal turn to the right, aligning with the runway, and take off, flying in a northwesterly direction.

In a loose trail formation, with the sniffer Huey in the lead, the helicopters level out at 1,500 feet altitude and fly toward the "Wagon Wheel." This well-known landmark is formed by the convergence of six straight canals that look like the spokes of a wheel from the air.

About twenty minutes into the flight, they are flying over vast open areas of marsh and tall grasses in the southern portion of the Plain of Reeds. Looking southwest, Lake can see the "Wagon Wheel" approximately ten klicks (six miles) in the distance. Moments later, he sees the C&C Huey approaching head-on from the west.

Flying the C&C Huey, Fuller swings slightly south, making a wide, left-hand, 180-degree turn to join the group of five helicopters. Coming alongside, Fuller places a radio call alerting the troop that they are near the operations area.

Hearing this, Ace and his wingman reposition their aircraft, closing in behind the sniffer Huey. The Cobra Gunships take a covering position well behind and above the three aircraft.

With the Scouts in position, Fuller places another radio call. "Longknife Two-Eight, you are clear to deploy along the canal to your twelve o'clock."

SNIFFER CRASH

Lake makes a slight course correction with the cyclic control to line up on the canal. Then he lowers the collective to begin his descent at five hundred feet per minute.

Moments later, the Huey starts shaking violently. The vibration is so severe that Lake cannot read the instruments on the panel in front of him. His aircraft has experienced a tail rotor failure. Ken attempts to turn the aircraft to the left and finds the controls unresponsive. The disabled Huey with no anti-torque control starts spinning.

Following close behind, Cozzalio sees the Slick's nose pitch up and then swing down as it starts spinning to the right, headed for the ground. Spinning slowly at first, the Huey spins faster and faster as it plummets downward. Stunned by what he is witnessing, Ace follows the disabled aircraft as it spins toward its obvious demise.

Other pilots watch in dismay. Some attempt to offer advice on the radio: "Maintain your airspeed" and "Lower the collective." But there is no advice that can help this ill-fated aircrew.

Somehow, one of the Huey pilots manages to level the aircraft and stop the spinning just before it slams into the ground. The aircraft hits flat on the skids, and the tail boom separates, collapsing to the ground. Smoke and flames erupt from the engine compartment.

"I dove after it," said Ace, "and I'm about one hundred feet off the ground when the Huey impacts and explodes."

RESCUE

Ace lands his Loach in the tall elephant grass on the right side of the burning Huey and rolls the OH-6 throttle to flight idle. He tells his crew chief, Wilt, to grab the fire extinguisher as they both scramble to exit the helicopter.

Disregarding the intense heat and risk of explosion, they sprint to the crashed aircraft. "Chamberlain was the first there and began spraying the fire extinguisher on the pilots and the area around them," said Cozzalio.

Brock McCloskey, the copilot, sitting in the right seat, is momentarily knocked unconscious from the impact. He later reports awakening to find himself engulfed in flames. Panic-stricken, he tries to get up but is restrained by his safety harness. He thinks, "I gotta get out of here." The windscreen and instrument panel, normally in front of him, are gone. The helicopter's skids are spread, and the belly of the Huey is embedded in the mud. He quickly releases his seat belt and takes two steps straight out the front of the aircraft. He continues another five steps and hears someone yell, "Get down." Thinking they are receiving enemy fire, he dives for the ground.

Hanging limp against his safety harness, Ken Lake, the aircraft commander, is unconscious, but alive. By now the fire is intense with flames licking around his seat. Ace probes and is unable to locate the lap release on Lake's safety harness. Using his knife, he slices rapidly on the thick webbing as the fire burns his forearm. Eventually, Lake falls free and Ace pulls his limp body out of the aircraft, dragging him to safety.

In the meantime, Fuller lands the C&C Huey on the left side of the burning aircraft. As he rolls the throttle to flight idle, he sees Ace attempting to rescue the aircraft commander. Marvin exits his aircraft and runs to assist, making his way through the chest-high elephant grass. When he approaches the burning aircraft, he sees McCloskey jump to his feet in front of the Huey and wave his arms over his head. Fuller diverts his course to take care of the copilot. As he escorts McCloskey back to the C&C aircraft, Marvin can see he has suffered burns and is very pale, obviously in shock.

After rescuing the aircraft commander, Ace turns his attention to the crew and passengers. By this time, the fire is out of control and the passenger compartment is engulfed in flames. To his dismay, Ace is unable to get to the hopelessly trapped crewmembers. The crew chief, Sergeant Bruce Brogoitti; door gunner, Sergeant Donald Hawkins; and two sniffer operators, Sergeant First Class Ralph Milbourne and Staff Sergeant Victor Trujillo, perish in the fire.

MEDEVAC AND TREATMENT

As the Huey continues to burn, Ace and Wilt carry the dazed and injured Ken Lake to the C&C Huey. After carefully loading Lake, Fuller takes off and transports the two pilots to the 3rd Surgical

Hospital medical pad at Dong Tam. Upon landing, hospital medics place the two injured aviators on gurneys and wheel them into the emergency room for evaluation and treatment.

Brock McCloskey suffers severe burns and a broken collarbone. After a short stay in the Dong Tam hospital, he is medevaced to Clark Air Force Base Hospital in the Philippines and later to Japan for medical treatment. After recovering from his injuries, he is assigned to Fort Eustace, Virginia, where he continues flying helicopters. Later, he receives a commission to first lieutenant and trains to fly Cobra gunships. He returns to Vietnam in 1971, flying with the 11th Armored Cavalry Regiment.

After several days in the hospital at Dong Tam, Ken Lake is transferred to the hospital at Navy Binh Thuy, near Can Tho, where he is treated for back injuries and a collapsed lung. After three weeks of recuperation, he is released from the hospital and returns to D Troop. Ken continues flying Slicks and becomes one of the most proficient and well-respected aircraft commanders in the Longknife Lift Platoon.

Ace and Wilt fly back to Camp Bearcat. Cozzalio goes to the infirmary, where he receives treatment for burns to his forearms. He is released and returns to the troop area.

When interviewed for *The Old Reliable*, the 9th Infantry Division newspaper, Ace said, "My crew chief, Wilt, deserves all the credit. He really hustled under pressure." [14]

SOLDIER'S MEDAL

On September 20, 1968, Ace Cozzalio and William Chamberlain are awarded the Soldiers Medal for heroism not involving combat.

This is a very prestigious award. Army Regulation 600-8-22, paragraph 3-14 states, "The performance must have involved personal hazard or danger and the voluntary risk of life under conditions not involving conflict with an armed enemy. Awards will not be made solely on the basis of having saved a life." It is the highest honor a soldier can receive for an act of valor in a noncombat situation, held to be equal to or greater than the level that would have justified an award of the Distinguished Flying Cross had the act occurred in combat.

CAUSE OF THE CRASH

The aircraft accident report determined that a tail rotor drive shaft failure caused the crash. While undergoing maintenance the night before the flight, a ball peen hammer was left inside the open tail rotor drive shaft cowling. Later, someone closed the cowling, leaving the hammer inside. The hammer, rubbing against the drive shaft, caused metal fatigue and eventually the shaft severed. When the tail rotor failed, the Huey encountered severe vibration; the airspeed decreased and the aircraft entered a right-hand spin.[15]

CHAPTER 12

WARWAGON RECRUITS

THE INTERVIEW

WHEN VACANCIES EXIST IN THE Warwagon Platoon, Ace seeks to enlist new pilots to fly Scouts. Realizing that the new Loach pilots will eventually serve as his wingmen, he undertakes this role with great forethought and deliberation. Selecting the right person could become a life or death decision.

Observing the troop newbies, he keeps an eye out for single men who demonstrate they are not only good pilots but also have the "balls" to take the necessary risks of flying low level and engaging the enemy face-to-face. Once he identifies a potential candidate, he approaches him, asking if he would like to be considered for the Scout Platoon. A positive response results in an interview in the O-Club, where Ace expounds on the honor and privilege of flying with the Warwagons. He leads the newbie to think he was selected from among a group of several elite candidates, when in actuality he may have been the only candidate. After a lengthy explanation of what it takes to fly Scouts, Ace tells the new recruit he passed the "test" and is now a Warwagon. He wraps up the interview with "Be at the flight line tomorrow at 0600 hours, ready to take your check ride."

WINSETT—"HE AIN'T FLYIN WITH ME"

Like most newbie pilots, Warrant Officer Gary Winsett is initially assigned to the Longknife Platoon, flying Slicks. This gives the new pilots an opportunity to familiarize themselves with the area geography, mission roles, and radio procedures. On Winsett's first mission, he is assigned to fly peter pilot (copilot) for First Lieutenant Jim Clary. Clary is section leader for the Longknives and is flying chalk one (lead) in a flight of three Hueys inserting eighteen Doughboys.

Gary is quick to admit, "I have no idea what is going on. I am essentially dead weight occupying the right seat." The initial part of the mission is uneventful; the Doughboys are inserted and retrieved several times during the day. Toward the end of the afternoon, things suddenly change when the Longknife Slicks return to extract the Doughboys.

Winsett describes what happens. "We make our approach to the LZ and start taking hostile fire. Our door gunners are shooting their M-60s, and the Cobras are blasting our flanks with rockets. Explosions and gunfire are all around us. Clary is on the controls. Those Longknives have great discipline. They don't talk, they don't bullshit, they don't chatter—they just keep flying."

The three Hueys, in trail formation, settle into the LZ, coming to a hover above the rice paddy. The Doughboys run to the waiting aircraft and scramble to climb aboard as enemy AK-47 fire splashes in the muddy water around them. The door gunners are returning fire, shooting their M-60s with a continuous *Rat-tat-tat-tat-tat-tat-tat-tat*. The Cobras attack the tree line. The *THUMP, THUMP, THUMP* of rocket explosions and *BRRRRRRRRRRRRRRRIP* of minigun fire is pervasive.

Winsett continues, "I suddenly realize we're in combat, we're getting shot at! I'm looking out and I see a bad guy running in the tree line. I draw my .38-caliber revolver and lean out the window firing six shots at the guy in the woods. Clary starts screaming at me, 'What the hell are you doing?' He chews my ass. Nobody told me I was supposed to be on the controls in case he got shot. I was a new guy. I thought I was supposed to be killing Communists."

Clary pauses his reaming of Winsett to announce on the radio, "Chalk one is up." That's followed immediately by "Two's up…. Three's up." Then Clary announces, "Slicks departing one niner zero." The three Hueys lift their tails and depart the LZ with the door gunners firing into the tree lines.

Upon their return to Camp Bearcat, the Longknives assemble in Lighthorse Operations for a debriefing. Winsett describes the scene. "It really wasn't a debriefing at all. I was in the dunce chair and all the 'old guys' chewed my ass. I heard, 'He ain't flying with me,' and 'What kind of pilots are they sending us these days?' It was hazing, and all I could do was sit there and take it." The "old guys" were unrelenting with their harassment, even though most were secretly thinking: I always wanted to do that myself.

"OUGHTA BE A SCOUT PILOT"

About that time, Ace Cozzalio walks by and Clary shouts, "Hey, Ace, we got John Wayne in here. We got a guy you need."

Ace asks, "What did he do?" Clary goes into great detail describing Gary's pistol shots at the VC in the woods. He expounds on how Winsett didn't follow protocol and what would have happened had Clary been wounded and Gary wasn't on the controls.

After listening to Clary, Ace turns to look at Winsett and says, "I'll take him. Sounds like he oughta be a Scout pilot."

Clary replies, "You can have him."

Ace motions to Winsett and says, "Come with me. You're moving to the Warwagons." Gary thinks to himself, "Sounds good to me. I'll do anything to get away from this bunch." As they walk to the Warwagon area, Cozzalio tells Winsett, "You wanta be in the Scout Platoon, you gotta be good. We don't take any deadwood. We don't take any castoffs."

After getting Gary settled in a Warwagon hooch, Ace tells Winsett, "Meet me at the flight line at 0600 hours to get checked out in the Loach."

CHAPTER 13

LOACH INSTRUCTOR PILOT

FLYING THE LOACH

IN ADDITION TO SECTION LEADER, Ace also serves as IP (instructor pilot) for the Warwagons. Having taught himself to fly the OH-6, he has a unique method of instructing new Scout pilots. Covering the basics of flying on the first day, he next dedicates several days of focused training on the armament system. Cozzalio believes that Scout pilots must have absolute familiarity with their weapons and learn the skills necessary to accurately fire the minigun. He expects the new pilots to hone their flying skills on their own, typically in the field, flying trail for Ace.

Day one: At 0600 hours, Gary Winsett meets Ace on the flight line in the Warwagon area. Cozzalio takes him to an OH-6 setting inside an L-shaped revetment made of sandbags stacked about four feet high. Together, they walk around the aircraft with Ace telling Gary to check this and check that. After about twenty minutes, Ace says, "OK, let's take her up."

With Winsett in the right seat and Cozzalio in the left, he instructs Gary on the startup procedures. Once the OH-6 is at operating rpm, Ace takes the controls and lifts the Loach to a three-foot hover. Sliding to the right, he moves away from the revetment and hovers to the runway. He brings the Loach to a stationary hover and tells Gary, "All right, you got it. Let's fly around the traffic pattern."

Having never flown an OH-6, Winsett takes the controls. Gary describes his flight. "I take off, climb to five hundred-foot altitude, and fly around the traffic pattern. I'm just putting along, doing eighty knots (ninety-two mph), thinking I am doing a great job. I turn to the final leg to make my approach to the runway, and I say to Ace, 'Sir, you want me to land to a hover or go to the ground?'" Cozzalio replies, "It don't matter; you're going to be dead by now flying like this."

Gary lands, and Ace takes the controls, saying, "I've got it. Let me show you how we do this." He lifts off with the skids about six inches off the ground and quickly accelerates to a hundred knots (115 mph). Then he announces, "We're going to keep a tight pattern," and slams the cyclic sharply left, making a tight left turn while maintaining about a hundred feet off the ground. He turns downwind, base leg and final approach while Winsett watches the airspeed indicator occasionally hit redline (152 knots [175 mph]). Gary says, "He drives that Loach hard and flares to land right on the spot he departed." Then Ace says, "That's how we fly. You do that Fort Rucker[ii] shit out there, and Charlie's gonna knock you out of the air. Now that's good for flight school, but it ain't worth a shit over here."

"Now you try it," says Ace. Gary takes the controls and flies faster and lower, trying his best to replicate what Ace showed him. He competes the traffic pattern and overshoots his landing.

Then Ace says, "All right, let's do an autorotation," meaning an emergency landing without power. Ace takes the controls and flies the traffic pattern, this time at five hundred feet. As he approaches the runway on the final leg, he rolls the throttle off, pushes the collective pitch control all the way down, and enters autorotation. Without power, the air moving upward through the rotor blades maintains rotor rpm as the helicopter glides downward to the runway. At about fifteen feet above the ground, he pulls back on the

---

ii   Fort Rucker is the home of the U.S. Army Aviation Center and School.

cyclic and flares the nose of the OH-6 upward while lifting the collective pitch control to slow the descent. As the Loach closes with the ground, he pushes the cyclic forward to lift the tail as the OH-6 settles softly onto the runway—a perfect autorotation.

"There, you try it," says Ace. Winsett takes the controls, climbs to five hundred feet, and does an autorotation that he later described as "uneventful."

"I've got it," says Ace. "Now here's what's probably gonna happen in the field." He takes off, flying about a hundred feet above the ground and goes way past the end of the runway. Gary describes what happens next. "Ace turns around and comes back smokin', about one hundred to one hundred ten knots (115 to 127 mph). He chops the power, pulls the cyclic back, and we go straight up. The airspeed indicator drops to about ten knots (twelve mph). Then he pushes the cyclic forward, and we roll over into a perfect autorotation. Later the Army had a name for it—a speed reduction climb. But I always called it an Ace Autorotation."

Then Ace says, "You do one." Gary does a couple and afterward is hovering forward about ten knots (twelve mph) when Ace says, "you're probably going to get one of these." He chops the power, and Gary does a quick hovering autorotation. "If you get your ass shot," says Ace, "you go down right where you are."

They complete the morning doing several hovering autorotations. Then Ace says, "You go get something to eat and I want you to come back and fly in the traffic pattern the rest of the afternoon. Don't do any autorotations—just practice your approaches and decelerations."

Then Gary says to Ace, "What call sign do I use?"

Ace replies, "Bench left, so you're now Warwagon One-Three."

Gary says, "Good, that's my lucky number." He returns after lunch and flies all afternoon. "I'm up there having a great time," says Winsett. "Occasionally, I think I would like to fly by Jim Clary and say, 'Look at me, Jim, I'm flying by myself.'"

LOACH ARMAMENT

Day two: The next morning Winsett meets Cozzalio at the airfield hanger. Ace says, "I'm going to get you squared away on the minigun." Gary has no idea what to expect. He later comments, "This is brain surgery. We take that minigun apart and reassemble it time and time again. He shows me every part and asks me questions. He is intense! Ace says, 'This is your life—you are an extension of that minigun.' We do this over and over again all morning long until lunch. At one point, I leave to get a cup of coffee. When I return, Ace had taken the minigun apart and hid one of the parts. Then he asks me, 'What's missing?' I look at all the parts laid out, and finally I identify it. Then Ace says, 'What's the name of that part?'"

After lunch, they return to the flight line and go to an aircraft. With the minigun unloaded, Ace simulates a jam, showing Winsett how to clear it. Then he shows Gary how to load the minigun by carefully placing the link ammo into the tray behind the seats, using dry graphite on the feed chute to keep the ammo moving smoothly.

After that, Ace climbs into the right seat. Grabbing the cyclic stick with his right hand, he explains, "When you pull the trigger to the first click, you fire two thousand rounds per minute. Pull harder to the second click, and you fire four thousand rounds per minute. The minigun has a six-second cutout to keep the barrels cool. When this happens, release the trigger momentarily and pull it again."

Ace tells Gary, "Climb in. Now we're going to do some shooting." Ace starts the Loach, comes to a three-foot hover, and lifts off, heading for VC Island, an uninhabited stretch of land in the middle of the Mekong River near Dong Tam. Using grease pencil marks on the windscreen as weapon sights, Cozzalio demonstrates how to fire the minigun. Diving the Loach at the island, he uses power and pitch to "aim the aircraft" as he fires into the sandy beach near the water. Winsett recalls, "Ace taught us to shoot over the bad guys and adjust our fire down upon them. That way they don't see it coming."

Then Ace demonstrates firing at a hover, using the foot pedals to adjust his fire laterally. He finishes a load of ammo and returns to Dong Tam to rearm. Then it's Gary's turn. They fly back to VC Island, and Winsett shoots a load of ammo with Cozzalio critiquing his technique.

Day three: Meeting at the hanger, Ace has Gary tear down and reassemble the minigun again. Then they go out and practice firing into VC Island. When they return, Ace says, "We need to break down that M-60 machine gun. Your crew chief will normally handle this, but you need to know how to do it." They break it down and put it back together several times.

After lunch, Ace says, "You're on your own. Go out there and shoot 'em up. You rearm it yourself."

"I fly out and shoot up VC Island all day long," says Gary. "I'd come low level down the river and shoot into the island. I am having lots of fun. At the end of the day, I figure I know all I need to know. I feel I am ready to fly a mission. What little do I know...."

DOOR GUNNER

Day four: Just when Winsett thinks he is ready to fly a mission, he finds there is one more task required of new Scouts—flying door gunner. Gary is assigned to fly with Ace the following day.

In the light of early dawn, Cozzalio and Winsett do a quick preflight of the helicopter. Then Gary straps himself into the left seat and gets comfortable with the M-60 machine gun hanging from a bungee cord attached to the doorframe. Ace tells Gary, "You don't shoot until I tell you. And you be damn sure you don't hit my rotor blades."

Cozzalio starts the Loach, and they lift off, flying treetop level at about ninety knots (104 mph). Arriving at the AO, he starts scouting for any signs of enemy activity. Gary recalls, "I thought to myself, 'Ohhhhh shit, we're going to crash or hit a tree.' Ace was uncanny; he'd be looking one way and slam the cyclic the other way. I'm thinking, 'Wow, I have to learn how to fly like that.' I flew door gunner with him for eight or nine hours that day. At the end of the day I was bone tired, yet I couldn't wait to start flying on my own."

Winsett flies two more days as door gunner. The training Gary experiences is standard procedure for all new Warwagon pilots. Upon completion of this training, the new Scouts are cleared to fly a mission.

CHAPTER 14

FLYING TRAIL FOR ACE

THE RULES

NEW SCOUTS ARE ASSIGNED TO fly trail as Ace's wingman to "learn the ropes" before flying with other pilots. He has a strict set of rules for anyone flying his trail. Prior to taking off, Cozzalio meets with his wingman, giving him a pep talk on today's mission. Then he lays out the ground rules, saying, "You don't say shit on the radio. You didn't talk at all. The only words I want to hear from you are 'taking fire' or 'going down.' Your primary function is to cover me. You're not to scout, not to look around. Your sole purpose is to keep a gun on my aircraft at all times."

COVERING LEAD

Flying en route to the AO, Ace flies low level, less than fifty feet above the ground and ninety knots (104 mph) airspeed. He instructs his wingman to follow behind and constantly alternate his position from left to right behind the lead aircraft. The wingman is instructed to stay close but never lock into one position. Lead flies straight and trail follows, weaving from one side to the other. He believes this erratic pattern makes it more difficult for the enemy to fire at the Scouts, especially since they typically shoot at the second aircraft passing overhead.

Arriving at the operations area, Cozzalio descends to ground level and slows to look for signs of enemy activity. Most of Ace's scouting is less than thirty knots (thirty-five mph) airspeed. Since the minigun fires forward, and the crew chief covers the left side, the right side of the lead Loach is unprotected. Ace directs his wingman to fly approximately forty-five degrees off the right rear of his Loach. This positioning allows the trail's door gunner to cover the right side of the lead aircraft with his M-60 machine gun.

Not only does Ace teach the pilots, he also instructs the door gunners, telling them to "always be in position to shoot under my aircraft." He has found that the VC will remain hidden until the lead aircraft passes overhead before they expose themselves to shoot.

NEWKIRK'S FIRST MISSION

Warrant Officer David Newkirk recalls his first mission, flying trail for Ace. Like Winsett, this occurs after several days of intense weapons and flight training. "By this time, I am scared shitless of Ace," said Newkirk. "He keeps looking out his door and telling me I'm too far, too close, or not on the forty-five-degree angle." After several missions, David learns to keep his Loach in the proper position, forty-five degrees off the right rear of Cozzalio's aircraft.

One day, while flying a mission in Kien Hoa province, south of Dong Tam, Ace is flying about twenty-five knots (twenty-nine mph), scouting for the enemy along a wood line. After passing a group of trees on his left, a Vietcong soldier jumps to his feet and fires an AK-47 into the left side of Ace's Loach. Ace calls, "TAKING FIRE!"

Looking out his aircraft's left door, Newkirk sees the guy stand and shoot. He swings his Loach to the left and fires his minigun, killing the VC with a long burst. Later, Ace congratulates Newkirk for his first kill and, with a big grin on his face, says, "I should have got him."

Several days later, Cozzalio and Newkirk are flying a mission further south, near Tra Vinh, where they come upon a Vietcong flag flying on a tall pole in the middle of a field near a U.S. artillery firebase. It is likely the VC planted the flag during the night to harass the GIs in the firebase.

Ace flies to the flagpole and, after checking for trip wires or booby traps, he snags the VC flag on the tip of his helicopter's right skid and pulls it off the pole. Later, while refueling, Ace approaches Newkirk and hands him the flag, saying, "The lead man always gets the flag for his wingman." Newkirk is honored by Ace's gesture and still has his treasured war trophy today.

WINSETT'S FIRST MISSION

Winsett finally gets to fly his first mission—paired with Ace. He is both excited and apprehensive at the same time. Prior to the flight, Ace gives his usual pep talk and tells Gary, "Your job is to keep a gun on me at all times. And, if I go down, you better be flying through the wreckage to get me." Then he pauses and says, "Hey, you got a twenty on you?" Eager to please his leader, Winsett reaches in his pocket and pulls out a twenty-dollar MPC (Military Payment Certificate). Ace takes the twenty, puts it in his pocket, and says, "I'll pay you back. If I owe you twenty dollars, you'll come get me."

This first day's mission is uneventful. Nonetheless, it is a huge learning experience for Winsett. Gary is doing his best to cover Ace's every move. He recalls, "Occasionally I drift out and Ace hollers on the radio, 'One-Three, where are you? Get over here!'"

On the following day, Winsett is alternating from left to right behind Ace, who is flying low level en route to the AO. "All of a sudden I look up and Ace is vertical," says Gary. "He zooms that son of a bitch straight up. At the top, he does a pedal turn and rolls right, flying straight down and firing his minigun at a guy in a boat. I look at that maneuver and say to myself, 'Damn, I didn't know a Loach could do shit like that.' I get out of his way because I don't know what is going to happen next. I go into my left-hand turn, covering Ace's recovery at the bottom of his dive. My door gunner is shooting his M-60 at guys on the shore near the boat. We start a fight right there. The Cobras roll in and we begin working that river. We happen onto a good size group of bad guys and have a pretty good battle that day."

On yet another day, Winsett is covering Cozzalio when he starts firing into a bunker. Gary veers away and rolls into a left-hand circle, covering Ace. Then he sees Cozzalio do an incredible maneuver with a helicopter. "Ace rolls into the bunker, firing his minigun," says Winsett. "Then he stops, pulls back on the cyclic, lifts a little collective pitch, and backs out about a hundred feet while climbing. Then he rolls in again. He does this repeatedly, working that Loach like a saw, in and out, in and out, while firing his minigun into the bunker. I am amazed by his flying ability."

NEWKIRK'S LEAD

Ace has another rule that he is adamant about—the wingman never flies in front of the lead aircraft. NEVER!

David Newkirk has been flying trail about two months, and, in David's opinion, he is ready to fly lead. One morning, he and Ace return to Dong Tam to refuel. The refueling area has three small refueling pads in a row next to the large pads for the larger Chinook helicopters. Ace flies in with Newkirk trailing and lands on the middle pad. Newkirk, avoiding the Chinook pads, flies around and lands on the pad in front of Ace.

Cozzalio gets out of his aircraft and walks over to Newkirk's Loach. He grabs David by the chicken plate and says, "Where's your team integrity? I'm the lead; you're the trail. You never fly in front of lead. You want to lead? You're lead this afternoon." Cozzalio purposely selected the middle pad to set up Newkirk. He intended to check him out as lead and wanted to see how he handled the stress.

That afternoon Newkirk flies lead, and Cozzalio is on his case all afternoon. Ace calls David, saying, "What are you looking at? Come back over here. Slow your airspeed. You missed that bunker." By the end of the day, Newkirk is frazzled, but pleased to have completed a mission flying lead.

The following day Newkirk is assigned to fly lead with Winsett as his wingman, a pair that became a great scout team, thanks to Ace's training. And, as Winsett commented years later, "We had fun. We hit trees. We chased the VC. We were a badass scout team."

Through Cozzalio's efforts, the new Scouts learn to fly like Ace. And, in many respects, they assimilate Ace's focused determination to seek out and destroy the enemy.

CHAPTER 15

ACE CAPTURES VC

"Average intelligence and a lot of common
sense is a requirement for success."

—ACE COZZALIO

MANY "GREAT CANALS," FORMING LONG, narrow water highways, criss-
cross the Plain of Reeds. Traveling mostly at night, the Vietcong
and NVA use these waterways to transport their equipment, muni-
tions, and soldiers. During the daytime, they seek refuge in the
dense vegetation on either side of the canals. This tangle of trees,
vines, and undergrowth offers prime hiding places for the enemy
and their sampans. Thus, the Plain of Reeds waterways are recognized target areas for finding and engaging the Vietcong and
NVA. And, the Scout helicopters are ideally suited to seek out
the enemy's hiding places. What follows is such a mission that occurred in September 1968, when Ace takes a prisoner in a most
unusual manner.

VC IN THE WATER
Two Warwagon Scouts, with Ace Cozzalio in the lead, are flying
a recon mission along one of the long, straight canals west of Tan

113

An. The two Scouts fly in formation ten to fifteen feet above the water and cruise along at thirty to forty knots (thirty-five to forty-six mph). At times, Cozzalio will slow to inspect a suspicious area along the canal while his wingman flies a high left-hand circle covering him. This activity continues for mile after mile, and they haven't discovered anything suspicious.

Suddenly, Ace spots a military-age male in the distance, running down a path alongside the canal. This man appears to be carrying a weapon. Ace lifts the collective control and simultaneously pushes the cyclic forward to accelerate and take pursuit. As he closes on the suspect, he watches the man toss the weapon aside and jump into the canal, but he doesn't come up for air. Circling back, Cozzalio decides to land his Loach and attempt to find this guy, possibly taking a prisoner.

Ace lands on the earthen berm next to the canal and positions his Loach with its left side toward the water so his door gunner can cover him with the M-60 machine gun. He calls his wingman, telling him to land on the opposite side of the canal and, likewise, position his aircraft so his door gunner can provide covering fire if needed.

Rolling his aircraft's throttle to flight idle, Ace removes his flight helmet, dons his white Stetson, and climbs out of his Loach. Reaching inside the doorframe, he retrieves his Civil War–era cavalry saber and attaches it to the left side of his gun belt. Then he makes his way down the canal embankment and proceeds to the place where he saw the suspicious man jump into the water. With his right hand, he draws his saber and steps into the canal. As he slowly steps forward, he pokes the blade of the saber down into the water in front of him. He finds the bottom isn't hard—just mucky mud. He continues poking in the mud and moving about the area for five to ten minutes.

Then he hits something hard. Ace described what happened next: "I thought 'aha,' and push on the saber a little harder and the 'solid something' starts to move. I just kinda force the object up, you know, pulling the saber up in front of me while keeping pressure on the tip. Well, up out of the water comes this man." When asked how the guy was staying under water, Ace answered, "He had a reed in his hand and used the reed to breathe while lying on the bottom of the canal."

Ace Takes a Prisoner

As unlikely as it seems, Ace captures a suspected Vietcong soldier with his saber. With the tip of his saber pointed into the back of the man, he escorts his captured suspect back to his still-idling Loach. Using his limited Vietnamese vocabulary, he instructs the suspect to stand on the right side skids of the Loach just outside his door. Before they take off, Ace hits the man in the chest, knocking him to the ground, demonstrating that he can push the guy off if he tries anything. Then Cozzalio rolls the throttle to operating rpm and lifts off, taking his prisoner to Dong Tam. Upon arrival, Ace hands the suspect off to the 9th Infantry Division Military Intelligence group for interrogation.

When asked if they captured many prisoners, Ace replies, "Yeah, just to keep things interesting we had a little contest going in our Scout Platoon. Scouts could earn beer and soda credits by catching Dinks. If you recall, sodas and beer cost us twenty or twenty-five cents, real expensive. Whoever captured the most prisoners never had to buy anything at our little lounge for a month. We got pretty good at capturing prisoners."

Another Prisoner Story

On another day, Ace and his wingman are flying a mission east of Ben Tre in an area composed of mile after mile of bright green rice paddies. After scouting one area and finding nothing of interest, the air mission commander instructs the Scouts to relocate to another area several klicks to the south. The two Loaches turn south and climb to an altitude of three hundred feet. The Scout pilots jokingly refer to this as "nosebleed altitude."

Up ahead Ace sees a lone person in the middle of a rice paddy. When they get closer, he can see it is a military-age male carrying a rifle. Cozzalio radios his wingman and tells him he is going to drop down to check it out. Dropping out of the sky, Ace comes to an abrupt hover directly in front of the man who is standing in calf-deep water. He positions his aircraft with the minigun pointed at the suspect, and the crew chief leans out the left door aiming his M-60 machine gun at the perplexed Vietnamese. When faced with the heavily armed Loach, the guy stands in place with his arms extended upward and appears to Chieu Hoi (surrender).

Ace maneuvers his Loach to a position about ten meters away, finding a more appropriate place to set his aircraft down. About the time the skids touch the ground, the VC suspect tosses his rifle aside and takes off running across the rice paddy. "I get out of the helicopter and go after the son of a bitch," said Ace. "I finally have to shoot him with my 357." Apparently Ace cannot catch the guy and eventually draws his pistol and fires, creasing the suspect's torso on the right side.

Ace brings his prisoner back to the Loach and makes him stand on the skids between the minigun and the left side doorframe. His crew chief wraps his left arm around the suspect's neck and holds a pistol in his right hand aimed at the suspect's forehead. When Ace lifts off, his wingman takes this photo from above. If you look closely, you can see the crew chief's left arm around the prisoner's neck.

Prisoner on skid of Ace's Loach
Courtesy of Rex Cozzalio

CHAPTER 16

WILLIE PETE

"Out of every one hundred men, ten shouldn't even be there,
eighty are just targets, nine are the real fighters, and we are
lucky to have them, for they make the battle. Ah, but the
one, one is a warrior, and he will bring the others back."

—HERACLITUS[iii]

DONG TAM—SEPTEMBER 15, 1968

AT SUNRISE, A LIGHTHORSE CAV Team of eight helicopters departs
Camp Bearcat heading southwest. They fly at 1,200 feet and plan
to refuel at Dong Tam before proceeding to the mission area southwest of Ben Tre. When they pass north of My Tho, they encounter
heavy rain and limited visibility. The team drops low, beneath the
clouds, and flies at five hundred feet AGL for the last ten klicks
(six miles) to Dong Tam Airfield.

After landing and refueling their helicopters, the pilots reposition their aircraft and shut down, waiting for the weather to break.
Positioned alongside the runway are three Slicks, two Cobras, two
Loaches, and the C&C Huey. The pilots, crew, and eighteen troopers of the Doughboy Aero-Rifle Platoon pass the time, anxiously
awaiting the weather to clear.

---

iii Gary Winsett provided the Heraclitus quote that aptly describes Ace.

Seeking cover from the rain, some troopers sit inside the Hueys talking to their buddies while a couple of guys sit quietly in the jump seats, reading novels. Others seek the shelter of the roof overhang on a nearby building, where they can smoke a cigarette. Some of the Doughboys take time to double-check their weapons and equipment.

The more experienced troopers are somewhat nervous, but it is mostly due to the idle inactivity instead of the combat action they were expecting to encounter this morning. The new guys are showing signs of genuine concern. They have heard about the area near Ben Tre—a notorious Vietcong hotspot.

SCOUT THE LZ

At 1145 hours, the stormy weather has passed, leaving an overcast sky with a 1,500- to 2,000-foot ceiling and two miles visibility. After checking the weather forecast with the Dong Tam Control Tower, Major Duane Brofer approaches the troop and announces loudly, "Scouts and Guns, mount up. Let's move out."

The Crusader and Warwagon crews head for their aircraft and immediately go through the startup procedures. Soon they are in the air, headed south to the operations area where the Scouts will inspect and approve a landing zone for the Longknife Slicks to insert the Doughboys.

Flying at 1,200 feet altitude, Brofer, flying in the C&C Huey, arrives at the mission area about ten klicks (six miles) southwest of Ben Tre. Unlike the elephant grass swamps and rice paddies encountered elsewhere in the Delta, this area is different. Meandering streams intersect broad areas of tropical forests with dense vegetation, nipa palms, and coconut trees. Scattered throughout the vast forested areas are smaller open areas with knee-high grass and shrub brush. And, because of heavy monsoon rains, this area is very wet with standing water in most of the fields.

From high above, Brofer locates the dense woods where an enemy force is suspected to be operating. On the west side of the woods, the tree line is L-shaped with a large, open field extending to the west and north. He calls the Warwagon Scouts and directs them to inspect and clear a landing zone three hundred meters west of the wood line.

The Warwagon Scouts, with Cozzalio in the lead and Warrant Officer Bob Grove in trail, skim low across the treetops for several klicks as Brofer guides them to the prospective landing zone. Arriving at the open area, they drop to ground level and slow to twenty to thirty knots (twenty-three to thirty-five mph) as they fly around the eastern and southern perimeter of the open area, peering into the woods, looking for anything suspicious.

After inspecting the area for several minutes, Cozzalio calls Brofer, telling him the LZ is clear.

Brofer acknowledges and calls Longknife 26, telling him to load up and head for the operations area.

SEND IN THE DOUGHBOYS

Sitting in the lead Huey's pilot seat while listening to the radios, Longknife 26 turns and hollers to the other pilots, "It's showtime! Start your aircraft." The Longknife pilots and their crew scramble to their Hueys and immediately go through the startup procedure. Once the Slicks are at flight idle, the Doughboys grab their weapons and equipment and climb aboard. Soon, the flight of three Hueys is airborne, headed across the Mekong River to the south.

Ten minutes later, Brofer sees the three Hueys approaching from the north and calls Cozzalio, instructing him to "pop a smoke" in the landing zone.

Ace's crew chief pulls the pin on a smoke grenade and drops it in the southern end of the LZ. Ace calls, "Smoke's out."

From high above, Brofer calls, "Longknife Two-Six, the LZ is at your eleven o'clock and smoke's out."

Longknife 26 replies, "Roger that. I have purple smoke." Brofer replies, "Purple it is. You are cleared to land."

The three Slicks, flying in trail formation, adjust their course to the left and set up their approach. Not wanting to draw attention to their location, the door gunners, as instructed, do not to fire unless fired upon. Dropping low, they fly at eighty knots (ninety-two mph) airspeed, racing across the treetops until they break out over the long, open field with purple smoke streaming upward at the far end. Closing on the smoke, they flare to reduce their airspeed. Then, in a sequence less than a second apart, the three Slicks come to a hover in front of the purple smoke, now swirling sideways in the lead Huey's rotor wash.

With the aircrafts' skids dipping in the foot-deep water, the Doughboys jump off and hastily move away from the helicopters. Then, in unison, the three Slicks lift their tails as they depart the LZ to the south.

RECON IN FORCE

An enemy force of unknown size is suspected to be operating in this area. Sweeping eastward, the Doughboys' mission is a Reconnaissance in Force, seeking to engage the enemy.

> Reconnaissance in Force—A recon force that is large enough to fight a small battle, and is fast enough to maneuver out of the area if it encounters a force too big to handle. Their mission is to probe the enemy, gathering intelligence about its size and strength.

Crossing the wet, muddy, open area, the Doughboys enter the woods and continue eastbound. About forty minutes into the mission, they come upon an open field, approximately three hundred meters across and four hundred meters wide, with knee- to waist-high grass. In line formation, the eighteen troopers cautiously advance toward the wood line on the other side.

When the Doughboys get within seventy meters of the woods, they are attacked by a much larger contingent of the Vietcong entrenched in the brushy woods along the eastern perimeter of the open area. Taking cover in the tall grass, they return fire into the wood line. Each time they attempt to withdraw, the VC hit them with massive amounts of AK-47 and machine gun fire. The troopers are pinned down, unable to maneuver in any direction. The Doughboys' platoon leader calls the Lighthorse air mission commander (Brofer) requesting air support and extraction.

Brofer responds quickly, placing radio calls on the troop FM frequency. "Warwagon One-Zero, Lighthorse Six. I need you to recon the area and give me a sitrep [situation report]."

"On the way," replies Ace.

"Longknife Two-Six, return to the AO for a hot extraction."

"Roger that. Cranking now," replies Longknife 26. The three Longknife Hueys, on call at Dong Tam Airfield, start their turbine engines and prepare to return for the Doughboys.

In less than a minute, the Warwagon Scouts arrive on the scene. Cozzalio and his wingman make a low pass over the dense vegetation and observe a group of Vietcong soldiers moving laterally through the woods on the north side of the field with the obvious intent of encircling the pinned-down troops.

Cozzalio calls Brofer. "Six, Victor Charlie are flanking on the north. We will hit that side while the Guns attack on east."

Brofer replies, "Affirmative." Then he calls Crusader 36, instructing the Gunships to commence their attack to the north, breaking right to avoid the Warwagon Scouts on their left flank.

Moments later, the Crusader Gunships commence their attack on the east side of the open area. At the same time, Cozzalio and Grove fly north across the open area to commence their assault on the left flank. Flying at treetop level with miniguns and M-60s blazing, they attack in a face-to-face shootout with the maneuvering enemy soldiers. Facing massive amounts of enemy fire, their aircraft takes numerous hits from small arms fire. Ace and his wingman continue their attack, firing and dropping frag grenades—killing and wounding many of the Vietcong combatants.

After completing a couple of gun runs, Ace is concerned. The enemy force is much larger than expected. Cozzalio realizes that, while he might slow them down, he cannot deter the VC from maneuvering to encircle the open area. The Doughboys must pull back promptly.

COVER THE DOUGHBOYS

Ace swings his Loach to the left, flying low over the nipa palms. He calls Brofer. "Six, I'm going to cover the Doughboys while they pull back."

"Roger that," replies Brofer.

Returning to the open area, Cozzalio brings his Loach to a high hover above the pinned-down Doughboys. Using the anti-torque pedals, he swings the nose of the OH-6 left and right, firing the minigun into the VC-infested woods. From the left seat, his crew chief leans out the door, firing his M-60 machine gun. Grove, in the trail Loach, climbs to about seventy-five feet and circles wide around Ace and the Doughboys, while placing suppressive fire into the trees.[16]

On the ground, the Doughboys see Ace's Loach arrive overhead, coming to a ten- to- twelve-foot hover above them. In an instant, Cozzalio unleashes his minigun, and a steady stream of hot brass (expended ammo) comes raining down on the Doughboys. The platoon sergeant stands and hollers, "Move out, pull back," as he motions with his left arm, pointing to the tree line they recently departed.

Using Cozzalio's Loach as their shield, the Doughboys quickly pull back two hundred meters to a pick-up zone near the tree line on the far western side of the field. Then Ace breaks off from his hovering maneuver and rejoins Grove to cover the extraction.

About that time, the Doughboys hear the familiar *Wop, Wop, Wop, Wop, Wop* sound of Huey rotor blades in the distance. Three Longknife Slicks accompanied by another team of Crusader

Gunships approach from the north. Longknife 26 calls the Doughboy platoon leader. "Doughboy four-Six, Longknife Two-Six. I have three Slicks en route to your location. Pop a smoke."

One of the Doughboys pulls the pin on a colored smoke grenade and tosses it into the far end of the pickup zone. Doughboy 46 calls, "Smoke's out."

Now on final approach, Longknife 26 sees the smoke and calls, "I have red smoke." Doughboy 46 replies, "Rosey Red it is. Come get us out of here!"

WILLIE PETE SMOKE SCREEN

Meanwhile, Cozzalio and Grove circle left and line up on the south end of the tree line. At this time, both aircraft are low on ammo. Realizing they are ineffective in a shoot-out, Ace calls, "Three-Six, cover me. I'm going in with 'Willie Pete.'" Cozzalio, with Grove flying his right-side trail position, dives from three hundred feet, making a low pass in front of the enemy positions. The crew chiefs in the two Loaches drop a total of twenty-six white phosphorus grenades into the forward edge of the tree line. The brilliant flash and bursts of white smoke effectively conceal the pickup zone from the enemy. As soon as the two Loaches break left, four Cobra Gunships make alternating gun runs to keep the enemy's heads down while the Hueys extract the Doughboys.[iv]

The three Slicks, in trail formation, drop into the open area, flare to decelerate, and come to a hover in the pickup zone. The Doughboys scramble to climb aboard as the Longknife door gunners cover their flanks with M-60 machine gun fire. In unison, the three Hueys tuck their nose and quickly depart to the south. All Doughboys are retrieved with no casualties.

---

iv Details extracted from an audio recording Ace Cozzalio sent to his family in early October 1968.

The Cav Team regroups at altitude and flies to Dong Tam to refuel before their return flight to Camp Bearcat. While en route to Dong Tam, Brofer places a radio call to the 9th Infantry Division Headquarters reporting a company-size force of Vietcong at grid coordinates XS425266. On the following day, two infantry companies of the 9th Division Mobile Riverine Forces are airmobiled into the area.

For his extraordinary heroism in close combat against a Vietcong force, First Lieutenant Ace Cozzalio is awarded the Silver Star.

Troop Commander, Major Brennon Swindell
presenting the Silver Star medal to Ace Cozzalio
Ace is wearing his yellow scarf, white Cav hat and saber.
Courtesy of Rex Cozzalio

CHAPTER 17

THE INDIANS NICKED ME

TRA VINH—SEPTEMBER 25, 1968

FLYING LOW AND SLOW, ACE and his wingman, Warrant Officer Tom Boeshore, aka "Baby Son," are searching for enemy activity in a large area, approximately fifty klicks (thirty-one miles) southeast of Dong Tam. Situated along the coast where the Mekong River empties into the South China Sea, this area is a patchwork of bright green rice paddies separated by dikes and canals. The weather is fair with nary a cloud in the sky, and the wind is calm. It's a pleasant break from the rainy monsoon season that has just passed, making it a perfect day for hunting "Charlie."

Together the two helicopters fly along the perimeter of the open rice fields, peering into the dense vegetation that borders the paddies. They are searching for footprints, trash, bent grass… any sign of recent activity. After searching several areas and finding nothing of importance, they lift up to fifty feet and relocate to a new sector within their assigned operations area.

Having recently arrived in Vietnam, Warrant Officer Chuck Nole is a "newbie" assigned to the Warwagons. Like all new Scout pilots, Nole is required to fly in the gunner position for his first two missions. Today he is flying left seat gunner for Tom Boeshore, trailing Ace. Not only is this his first mission, it is Nole's first time to fire the M-60 machine gun from a helicopter.

Upon entering the new sector, the two Loaches drop to three to five feet and start scouting the area. Minutes later, they come upon a large rice paddy intersected by a dike. The dike runs to a small island in the middle of the rice paddy. There, surrounded by a group of nipa palm trees, is a lone hooch.

The Hooch

Suspicious of the hooch, Ace makes a radio call to Boeshore. "Warwagon One-Two, cover me while I check this out." He flies to the middle of the rice paddy and circles the hooch, looking for anything out of the ordinary. Then he lifts up and hovers about ten feet above the hooch. Suddenly, without any communications, Ace stands his Loach on its nose and unleashes his minigun into the hooch, ripping it apart. Out the backside runs a man with a rifle slung over his shoulder, heading for the distant tree line. Ace calls out, "I'M HIT," and veers away from the hooch.

Circling the hooch about thirty yards away is Boeshore, covering Ace. When he sees the guy running, he pushes the cyclic forward with his right hand while simultaneously pulling in power with the collective in his left hand. The Loach lifts its tail as it takes pursuit.

"We chase this guy across the rice paddy with me firing the M-60," said Nole. "Bullets are spraying everywhere and we never hit that guy. He makes it to the tree line and gets away." Uncertain about Ace's situation, Boeshore breaks off and circles back to locate Ace.

Ace Is Hit

In the shootout, Ace is hit by an AK-47 round—the bullet grazing the left side of his neck. His Loach takes multiple hits in the engine compartment, and oil is spraying into the cockpit. Undaunted, Ace flies his Loach to an open area, lands in a rice paddy, and gets out to assess the damage. His aircraft has suffered several hits and, with the engine leaking, it is unflyable. His crew chief takes a bandage from the first aid kit and applies it to the large gash that, to their amazement, is bleeding minimally. All the while, they are taking sporadic fire from the enemy in a distant tree line with the rounds splashing in the rice paddy water around them.

Help on the Way

Crusader 36, flying a Cobra gunship, is air mission commander for today's mission. He places an open call on the troop FM radio frequency requesting a Longknife Slick to extract the Warwagon crew and their equipment.

Returning to Dong Tam in a D Model Huey, Warrant Officers Ken Lake and Gary Winsett hear a radio call on the troop push indicating that Warwagon 10 (Ace Cozzalio) is down. Lake immediately banks left, knowing precisely where the event is taking place. He makes a radio call to announce they are on the way and tells his crew to prepare for a "hot extraction."

Several minutes later, Lake spots the downed Loach in the distance and commences his approach. "Ken was a wizard flying that D Model," recalls Winsett. "He came in hot, made one turn, flared, and set that Slick down between the bad guys in the tree line and the Loach crew." Meanwhile, Lake's door gunner lays down suppressive fire with his M-60 machine gun while the Cobras make successive gun runs on the tree line.

At the Loach, the crew chief is scrambling to remove the minigun, radios, grenades, and other equipment from the disabled aircraft. Seeming in no particular hurry, Ace puts on his silver belly Cav hat, gathers his saber, helmet, and logbook, and saunters along a dike to the waiting Huey. Winsett recalls, "Ace comes walking to the Slick in that trademark stroll of his while pointing at his neck. Then he would stop and point at the tree line as if he was directing the air strike on the sniper fire. What a character!"

Arriving at the Huey, Ace has a broad smile as he climbs in the cargo compartment, taking a seat against the rear bulkhead. The bandage on his neck shows traces of blood, and Ace seems happy—apparently because the bullet only grazed him, and he earned his "red badge of courage."

JUST LIKE THE "OLD CAV"

Winsett recollects, "As soon as Ace got in the Slick, he put his helmet on and plugs into the Huey's intercom system. He announces, 'It was just like the old Cav—hit in the neck by a flaming arrow.'" Then he tunes to the troop push and announces, "Hey, Baby Son, don't worry, it's not a big deal. The Indians got me—but they just nicked me." When Boeshore and Nole hear this, they crack up. Ace is irrepressible.

Once the Loach crew and equipment are loaded in the Huey, Lake lifts off and heads back to Dong Tam. Landing at the 3rd Surgical Hospital medical pad, Ace is taken inside and treated for his wound. Later that evening, he leaves the hospital and catches a ride back to Camp Bearcat with a large bandage on his neck.

GROUNDED

Due to his injury, Cozzalio is grounded from flying until his wound heals. This doesn't sit well with Ace—he yearns to be in the air and misses the daily excitement of flying with the Cav. To pass the time, he spends most of his day in the Lighthorse Operations Center, listening to the troop radios, staying on top of the daily missions.

CHAPTER 18

WARWAGON AIR STRIKE

"If you are living, you might as well be alive."

—ACE COZZALIO

PLAIN OF REEDS—OCTOBER 1968

IN THE WEEK FOLLOWING ACE getting shot, Warrant Officer Chuck Nole is relaxing in his hooch on a down day. Suddenly, Ace Cozzalio storms into his room. He has a large bandage on his neck and announces, "Man, we got a mission, we got a mission." It doesn't matter that he is grounded from flight duty until his wound heals—he is determined to get back in the air. Ace tells Nole, "Come on man, let's go."

A Battalion of 3rd Brigade, 9th Infantry Division is in contact with the enemy north of Tan An. Using the landline telephone, the 3rd Brigade Tactical Operations Center calls Lighthorse Operations Center at Camp Bearcat requesting air support. Unfortunately, D Troop is on a mission elsewhere in the Delta and cannot respond. Looking for any opportunity to fly, Ace decides he will take the mission himself.

Nole grabs his helmet and flight gear and follows Ace to the flight line at the Camp Bearcat Airfield. On the way, they round up their crew chiefs. After a quick pre-flight, they crank their aircraft, and the two Scout pilots take off, heading south with no supporting gunships.

Once the Warwagon aircraft are within radio range, Cozzalio contacts the Battalion Operations Center and tells them that two Warwagon Scouts are on the way. He inquires about gunship support and is told the Stingrays, Bravo Company, 9th Aviation will meet them on location. At this point in time, the Stingrays are still flying Charlie Model Huey gunships. Now this might concern some Scout pilots, since they are accustomed to working with Cobra gunships, but it seemingly doesn't bother Ace.

LOACH PATROL

Flying to the south, the two Scouts arrive at the operations area about twelve klicks (7.5 miles) north of Tan An. Ace contacts the battalion commander, flying in a C&C Huey high above his infantry companies. He reports one of his companies is in contact with a large contingent of the Vietcong embedded along the Kinh Bo Bo Canal, one of the long, narrow canals that are prevalent in the Mekong Delta. He asks the Warwagons to scout the canal line and engage the VC should they make contact. Any personnel in this area are to be considered hostile and dealt with accordingly.

Ace inquires about the Stingray Gunships and finds they are tied up in another skirmish and will arrive later. Ace tells the battalion commander that the Warwagon Scouts will initiate their recon of the area without gunship support. Then he calls Nole on the troop push and announces, "Screw it! I don't care about that. Let's go."

The Kinh Bo Bo Canal is one of the many "great canals" excavated by the French colonial government in the late 1800s. It runs straight as an arrow for twenty-six klicks (sixteen miles) in a northeasterly direction from a point about nine klicks (six miles) north of Tan An Army Airfield. What makes this canal so distinctive is its crystal-clear blue water, unlike the muddy canals and streams found elsewhere in the Delta.

Soon, the two Scout pilots see a long, blue canal at their twelve o'clock. Flying in a southerly direction, the two Loaches descend and level out at fifteen feet above the canal, flying at thirty to forty knots (thirty-five to forty-six mph) airspeed. Focusing on the left flank where the enemy was earlier reported, the crew chiefs turn sideways in their seats and lean partially out the door, scanning the dense vegetation along the banks of the canal, searching for any sign of enemy activity. Ace scans the area ahead on both sides of the canal, hoping to find the enemy before they see the Scouts. After flying several miles, they haven't seen anything suspicious.

Suddenly, Nole, who is flying in the wingman position on the right side of Ace's Loach, sees something. "It is the first time, as a Scout pilot, that I find something significant," says Nole. "A guy swims underwater across the canal in front of me. I can see the mud he is kicking up in the clear water." Nole radios Ace, telling him about the guy underwater. They bank right, away from the canal, and circle back.

As the two aircraft line up on the canal, Ace calls, "I see it." He starts firing his minigun into the water. At that instant, they receive massive amounts of enemy fire from the tree line along the east side of the canal.

"I hear this popping sound," said Nole. "I am so new that I don't realize I am being shot at." The Scouts immediately return fire and become engaged in a shooting contest with the Vietcong in the woods along the canal.

WWAS

After shooting the man in the water, Ace makes another sweeping right turn, this time gaining altitude as Nole follows, mimicking his every move. Ace announces on the radio, "Whiskey, Whiskey,

Alpha, Sierra." Unbeknownst to Nole, this is code for a Warwagon air strike. From three hundred to four hundred feet altitude, the two Scouts roll in with miniguns blazing and the crew chiefs hanging out the left door firing their M-60 machine guns.

"It is like a mini Cobra gun run," said Nole, "only we are doing it from three hundred feet." After several WWASes, the two Loaches are low on fuel and ammo. Ace calls the battalion commander, telling him they are headed to Tan An to rearm and refuel.

Yeah, We Took a Few Hits

The two Scouts depart to the south. After receiving clearance to land from the Tan An Control Tower, they make their approach and come to hover in the middle of the airfield. After a pedal turn to the left, the two Loaches hover to the refueling area and set down on adjoining pads. As they refuel their aircraft, they assess their damage. Nole is surprised to find he has bullet holes all over his helicopter—the tail boom, rotor blades, and fuselage. Likewise for Ace, but it comes as no surprise to him.

Shortly thereafter, the battalion commander's C&C Huey arrives and sets down on a nearby refueling pad. The infantry battalion commander, a lieutenant colonel, walks over to thank the two Scout pilots, saying, "Man, I want to thank you guys. You saved the day for my ground troops." Then he glances over at the two Loaches and says, "Holy crap, what happened?"

Ace is quick to respond. "Oh yeah, we took a few hits. It's not a big deal. But we did find the bad guys for ya, didn't we, sir?"

Nole reflected later, "There I was, a wobbly one [warrant officer 1], not knowing what I am doing and my platoon leader has a big bandage on his neck—grounded, but flying anyway. Oh well, on that day we were heroes for the infantry battalion, and that's all that mattered."

Ace was hard on aircraft, especially in terms of battle damage. It wasn't because he was a "magnet-ass," as some unlucky aviators were called. It was due to Ace's aggressive style; he always sought out and took on the enemy face-to-face. On more than one occasion, Ace was overheard saying, "I like to get in close."

CHAPTER 19

ACE IS HARD ON AIRCRAFT

MOVE TO DONG TAM

IN AUGUST 1968, THE 9TH Infantry Division relocated its headquarters from Camp Bearcat to Dong Tam. And, in October, after completion of barracks and other troop structures, D Troop, 3-5 Cavalry, likewise, relocated their operations to Dong Tam.

Situated five miles west of My Tho, Camp Dong Tam was built up by dredging sand and silt from the Mekong River. On the newly created land, the Army Corps of Engineers constructed a base camp approximately one square mile in size with roadways, a thousand-foot runway, a huge heliport, a hospital, unit offices and billets, a Post Exchange, parade grounds, a golf course, a rifle range, a POW compound, and a reinforced defensive perimeter.[17]

From its new home base, D Troop is better situated to support the 9th Infantry Division conducting operations throughout the Mekong Delta. Strategically, the relocation to Dong Tam is a smart move—basing out of Dong Tam means shorter en route flying time and more combat time on station before refueling.

For Ace, he is very familiar with the geography around their new base camp. That familiarity gets him in trouble with his commanding officer shortly after relocating to Dong Tam.

Major Brofer

Major Brofer, Lighthorse troop commander, has a lot of respect and admiration for Ace. He is quoted in a press release, which reads: "Cozzalio is the very best I have seen," said Major Duane R. Brofer, Cozzalio's commanding officer. "You can't expect someone as legendary as Ace never to have taken a risk or brushed with death. It doesn't happen that way over here. He's good because he takes calculated chances. He, believe it or not, is the safest pilot I have. That is what makes him great instead of good."[18]

Even though Brofer viewed Ace as his best Scout pilot, he also had a realistic expectation about the use of the troop's aircraft.

Ace said, "Brofer used to get real pissed sometimes." He would say, "Damn it, Ace, what do ya think, we got a pipeline for these aircraft?"

The New Loach

It is October 1968 and Ace has flown combat missions for more than nine months. He has achieved astonishing combat results, yet his "close-in" action has taken a toll on the troop's aircraft. He was shot down by enemy gunfire six times, not to mention the many incidents when his Loach was so damaged from enemy fire that it was unflyable.

Shortly after their relocation to Dong Tam, D Troop receives a brand new OH-6 helicopter with only four hours on the airframe. When Ace sees the shiny new aircraft sitting in the maintenance area, he wants to be the first to fly it. He climbs into the right seat, puts on his helmet and gloves, and starts the engine. He thinks to himself, "Boy, this is awesome; the engine fires up quickly and runs smoothly. The rotor blades are in perfect sync with little to no vibration." He centers the cyclic and pulls up on the collective control while applying left pedal, bringing the OH-6 to a hover. Checking the controls, he does a right pedal turn and then a left pedal turn. Satisfied that everything is working properly, he hovers the new aircraft out to the Dong Tam runway and calls the control tower for takeoff clearance.

Receiving clearance to take off, he pushes the cyclic forward and lifts the collective. The new Loach lifts its tail and quickly accelerates to eighty knots (ninety-two mph) as he flies down the long runway, about four feet off the ground. Reaching the end of the runway, he swings the cyclic left to make a climbing left turn, all the time thinking, "Man, this aircraft flies like a dream." After flying around the traffic pattern at a hundred feet altitude, he lands to a hover in the middle of the runway. Doing a left pedal turn, he hovers to the maintenance area and sets the aircraft down.

Ace is excited about the new Loach and anxious to fly it on a mission. After shutting down the engine and securing the new OH-6, he walks over to the maintenance office and talks to a sergeant, making arrangements to have a minigun mounted that evening so he can fly it the following day.

FINDING THE "BOYS"

At this time in Ace's tour, he has flown many missions and is very familiar with the Mekong Delta. He has a pretty good idea of where the "bad guys" are hiding and looks for opportunities to find and confront them.

On the following morning, Ace proudly takes off in his brand new Loach. In a way, he feels like a teenager with his first car. Initially, he babies the new aircraft, proud to be flying such a fine piece of precision equipment, but that soon changes.

Today's mission takes the Cav Team across very familiar terrain southeast of Dong Tam. Ace tells the story of what happens next. "On the way to a mission, I know where some of the boys [VC] are hiding out, so I drop by to see them. Damn, they are out, so we have a little face-to-face and shoot the shit out of each other." Ace continues, "Well, they shot the shit out of this new aircraft. I hadn't been gone from our base camp for more than thirty minutes and come back leaking fuel and a lot of bullet holes."

Upon his return to Dong Tam, Ace takes the new Loach to maintenance for repairs. Then he checks out another OH-6 and returns to the operations area to resume the mission.

Note: It is a constant challenge for the Scavengers (Lighthorse Maintenance Platoon) to keep the troop's aircraft flying. At the end of each day, damaged aircraft are sent to the maintenance hangar, where crews work throughout the night making repairs to get the aircraft ready for the following day's mission.

CO GROUNDS ACE

Returning to Dong Tam that evening, Ace is shutting down his aircraft when he receives a message to report to the troop commander's office. Grabbing his flight gear and helmet, he heads for D Troop Headquarters.

Ace enters Major Brofer's office and, after giving a hand salute, says, "Sir, you wanted to see me?" Brofer returns the salute and replies, "I saw that new Loach you flew this morning, and frankly you made a mess of that new aircraft. You screwed up. You get to fly with the troop for a week." Ace knows better than to provide excuses or otherwise comment. He replies, "Yes, sir," does an about face, and departs the CO's office.

Years later when talking about this incident, Ace commented, "Damn, we think that is terrible. Flying ash and trash for a week!"[v]

It is apparent that Major Brofer knows exactly what reprimand will have the most impact on Ace and the other Scout pilots.

---

v Ash and trash: noncombat Huey mission carrying ammo, supplies, or personnel

CHAPTER 20

ACE AND FRANK

"Remember that the past is over and the future
is promised to no one, so work and play, living in
the present, and be grateful for your gains."

—ACE COZZALIO

BEST BUDDIES

ACE COZZALIO AND FRANK BRYAN were roommates while student pilots attending U.S. Army Primary Helicopter School, Class 67-18 at
Fort Wolters, Texas. Like Ace, Frank attended Officer Candidate
School and was commissioned a second lieutenant prior to flight
school. They soon became close friends, a friendship that endured
and strengthened during their time in Southeast Asia.

Arriving in Vietnam, Frank is assigned to B Company, 9th
Aviation Battalion, flying Charlie Model Huey gunships out of
Camp Bearcat. Having the same base camp, they see each other frequently and share stories about their flying experiences.
Impressed with Ace's stories about the air cavalry, Frank requests a
transfer to D Troop. In June 1968 his request is approved, and he is
assigned to the Crusader Gunship Platoon, flying AH-1G Cobras.

Ace and Frank are delighted to be in the same air cavalry troop.
They fly together on many missions, with Ace flying lead Scout for

the Warwagons and Frank covering him from above in a Cobra gunship. They share many adventures and a few mishaps, all serving to strengthen the bond between the two "Cav pilots."

Frank Bryan and Ace Cozzalio
Courtesy of David Conrad

In October 1968, Ace and Frank discuss the reality of their one-year Vietnam tour coming to an end and jointly decide to request an extension. They have a strong bond with the cavalry, have many close friends in D Troop, and, most importantly, they don't want to leave the daily excitement of flying with "The Cav." They both are approved for a six-month extension of duty in Vietnam.

R&R

Soldiers extending their tours are entitled to one month R&R. On December 9, 1968, Ace and Frank depart Vietnam and return stateside. Evidently, the two amigos blaze their way across several cities in the U.S. There are stories of their partying in San Francisco, Los Angeles, Sacramento, Denver, and Kansas City, Missouri. And, after visiting Frank's family in Lynn, Alabama, they attend David Conrad's wedding in Enterprise, Alabama. David, who completed his one-year Vietnam tour in early December, returned stateside, and is married on December 20.

Upon their arrival in California, Ace's girlfriend and her sister meet Ace and Frank in San Francisco. The four friends spend five days partying in the City by the Bay before visiting Disneyland in Anaheim for several days. After being with the guys for over a week, the girls get bored (so Ace says jokingly) and fly home. After seeing the girls off at the airport, Ace and Frank head for Sacramento, California, to spend several days with Ace's family.

While there, the *Sacramento Bee* interviewed Ace for an article titled "Copter Pilot—Home On Leave—Says Vietcong Are On The Run." Here is an excerpt from that article together with the newspaper photo.

"Charlie is in bad shape. He's running, living in holes in the ground, lying in underground bunkers or crawling in the tree lines." This is the first hand, close-up view of 1st Lt. Allen Ace Cozzalio, who has lived up to his middle name as a member of a breed which has come into its own in the Vietnam War, the helicopter pilot.

He is home with his father, Mel Cozzalio, for a 30-day leave. Then he will return to Vietnam for a voluntary six-month extended tour of fighting duty. He looks forward to returning. He will be flying a Huey Cobra, an air gunship that unleashes devastating firepower. And, he is to be pro-moted to Captain.... [16]

Photo courtesy Rex Cozzalio
Taken by Sacramento Bee

After their Sacramento visit, the two Cav buddies travel to St. Joseph, Missouri, where they visit the Stetson Hat Company, maker of the renowned silver belly cavalry hats. Ace wanted to show his appreciation to Stetson for accommodating the special production of Lighthorse Cav hats. While there, Ace picks up a new silver belly Stetson for First Lieutenant Dennis Olson, a new Warwagon Scout pilot. When Ace returns to Dong Tam, he will present the silver belly Stetson with the crown fully extended. Dennis won't change it; he'll wear his hat "Hoss Cartwright" style.

During their visit in the Kansas City area, Ace and Frank meet two young ladies. They take their female companions to a fancy restaurant in the big city. Hoping to impress his date and his buddy, Cozzalio motions to the waiter, who promptly arrives tableside. Ace tells him he is buying drinks for everyone in the restaurant. The waiter departs and assembles the other waiters, telling them to take drink orders from everyone in the restaurant.

Ace smiles smugly across the table at his buddy Frank. Not to be outdone, Bryan calls the waiter over and announces he is paying for the meals for everyone in the restaurant. Then he looks across the table at his buddy, Ace. They both start laughing uncontrollably. It is uncertain whether this impresses anyone except the restaurant patrons, but Ace and Frank have a good time and spend a bundle of money for their night on the town.

After attending Conrad's wedding in Alabama, they head back to California for the return flight to Vietnam. On the way, Ace and Frank spend a couple of days in Denver. While there, they attend a party and meet some young ladies. Not wanting to get serious and to have some fun, they decide to use assumed names. Ace introduces himself as Marvin Fuller, Ace's hooch mate back at Dong Tam. Frank uses another D Trooper's name. They have a great time, party until the wee hours, and never think twice about their assumed identities.

Eventually, the two pals arrive at Travis Air Force Base, California, and board their return flight to Vietnam. Soon, they are back "in the saddle," flying missions for Lighthorse Air Cavalry.

While Ace is on R&R, Marvin Fuller completes his tour and departs Vietnam on December 22, 1968. Marvin reports to his next duty assignment at Fort Knox, Kentucky, where he attends the Armor Officer Advanced Course. One day, he receives a call from a young lady. She talks to Marvin like they are old friends and wants to reconnect. Fuller politely declines and, after hanging up the phone, has a good laugh, knowing exactly what happened.

1st Lt. Ace Cozzalio and Capt. Frank Bryan
On R&R in December 1968
Courtesy of Rex Cozzalio

CHAPTER 21

NO AMMO; TRY THE 357

"Your success is predicated upon high self-esteem and self-trust."

—ACE COZZALIO

SCOUTS TO GUNS

ACE MOVED FROM WARWAGON SCOUTS to Crusader Guns in mid-November 1968. His first duty as a Crusader was to attend the three-week in-country Cobra transition course at Bien Hoa. After completing the course, he departed on R&R with his buddy Frank. Returning to Lighthorse on January 9, Ace was designated Crusader Gunship platoon leader, and on January 27, 1969, he was promoted to the rank of captain.

BEN TRE—FEBRUARY 6, 1969

In early February, Lighthorse received "hot intel" about an enemy concentration northeast of Ben Tre along a canal joining the Mekong River. On several missions, the Warwagon Scouts found empty bunkers, campsites, a few sampans, and dim trails, but no Vietcong.

Ace in his AH-1G Cobra Gunship
Courtesy of Rex Cozzalio

The morning briefing on February 6 takes on a more serious note. During the night, a sizeable number of Vietcong were observed moving into the area. A Lighthorse Cav Team is dispatched to find and engage the enemy.

Flying lead Scout for the Warwagons is Warrant Officer David Newkirk. Flying Newkirk's trail is Warrant Officer Gary Winsett. A team of two Crusader Cobras accompanies them. Warrant Officer Bob Munhofen is flying lead Gun with Captain Ace Cozzalio in the front seat, copilot position. The C&C Huey and trail Gunship crew are unknown.

SCOUT RECON

The Scouts, Cobras, and C&C Huey lift off from Dong Tam and fly in an easterly direction along the southern bank of the Mekong River. After a short, ten-minute flight, they arrive at the operation area. The two Scouts fly low across the rice paddy and slow to investigate the tree lines near the canals while the Cobras fly a racetrack pattern high above.

After working this area for twenty to thirty minutes, the Scouts find little evidence of enemy activity. About this time, the Cobra wingman develops a mechanical problem. He and the C&C Huey depart to Ben Tre Airfield, leaving a single Cobra on station.

The two Scouts relocate further east and begin working a three- to five-acre rectangular rice paddy with streams running along the west, north, and east sides. On the western boundary, a small stream joins a larger canal running east to west. At this junction, in the northwest corner of the paddy, the Scouts find several bunkers and a couple of hooches. The bunkers have a good field of fire across the rice paddy and appear to be protecting the junction of the two canals.

As the two Loaches approach one of the hooches, a military-age male jumps up from his hiding place and runs to the other side of the hooch. The Scouts take pursuit. Grabbing a hidden rifle, the guy swings around and takes aim at Newkirk's Loach. Before he can pull the trigger, David's crew chief, Specialist 4 Killen, nails him with his M-60 machine gun. At that instant, the entire tree line comes alive, erupting with small arms fire from AK-47 and SKS rifles.

THE FIGHT IS ON

Newkirk calls "taking fire," and the two Loaches veer away with guns blazing. At the same time, the Cobra gunship dives from above with Munhofen firing rockets and Cozzalio swinging the nose turret left and right, firing the minigun and lobbing forty-millimeter grenades on the enemy positions in the tree line. Circling back, the Scouts continue to attack the tree line from below while the Cobra hits the woods from above. "Newkirk and I are swapping out engaging these guys," says Winsett. "The VC keep popping up everywhere."

The intense firefight continues until both Scouts have expended all ammo and have taken numerous hits from enemy fire. Likewise, the Cobra has expended its rockets and ammo. Cozzalio radios the Scouts, suggesting they come to altitude and return to Dong Tam to rearm and refuel.

Tamale

An Air Force forward air controller (FAC), call sign Tamale, is in radio contact with the Cav Team, monitoring its activity. He arrives overhead and talks to Newkirk on the radio, saying he will coordinate with U.S. Air Force fighter jets to continue the attack. Tamale asks the Scouts to mark the target before they depart. Newkirk agrees, saying he will drop a smoke grenade in the rice paddy on their departure.

Newkirk Crashes

Newkirk makes a wide, sweeping right turn to line up his approach, running across the rice paddy from west to east. A wide, wooded area with tall palm trees borders the western side of the rice paddy. Some of the palm trees have their foliage blown off and look like skinny telephone poles emerging from the woods. Residual smoke from the rockets and burning hooches lingers in the area and drifts slowly across the treetops.

Flying low, the two Scouts pass over the western wooded area. Suddenly, Newkirk sees muzzle flashes directly beneath his Loach.

"I look down between the pedals and there's a guy with an AK. He unloads it right into me," said David. "The first shot grazes the inside of my right knee and hits my forty-five-cal. pistol I have positioned between my legs. The next round goes right through the engine. I pull all the collective pitch I have just to get away. Then I hit a palm tree, and the helicopter tumbles end over end before I crash in the rice paddy."

The disabled Loach hits hard and rolls, coming to rest in a tail-high position with the nose stuck in the rice paddy mud. The rotor blades, twisted and mangled, are drooping over the fuselage and the tail boom is missing.

Winsett, seeing Newkirk crash in front of him, makes a tight 360-degree turn to the right and sets down behind the crash, facing eastward. By the time Gary lands, both Scout crews are taking small arms fire from the tree line on the north and northwest.

FAKE GUN RUN

From the air, Munhofen and Cozzalio see the crash. They immediately dive toward the tree line. Since they have no ammo, they are hoping their "fake gun run" will keep the VC's heads down. After the first pass, the Vietcong resume firing. It is apparent that the Scouts on the ground need help and the mock gun run isn't working.

Ace says to Bob, "Well, this isn't working. We have to land down there and try to get them out ourselves."

Meanwhile, Winsett, having lost his radio to a bullet, is unable to contact Munhofen and Cozzalio in the Cobra gunship. His Loach, positioned between Newkirk and the west tree line, is a prime target for the Vietcong in the wood line. He looks to the east and sees the Cobra coming in fast and low. His initial thought is "Oh no, they are crashing, too." Then he notices the nose turret moving in all directions but no shots fired as they pass low over the rice paddy in front of the woods.

Soon, the Cobra returns, flares to slow, and comes to a hover between the crash site and the enemy positions in the tree line.

COBRA COVER BLUFF

As soon as the Cobra arrives on the scene, all firing ceases—it is strangely quiet other than the engine and rotor noise emitting from the two helicopters. Munhofen hovers the Cobra back and forth in front of the Scouts. Cozzalio is swinging the nose turret side to side, aiming the minigun at the tree line. Then one of the Vietcong, about a hundred yards away, emerges from behind a tree and starts taking pot shots at the Cobra. Ace aims the minigun at him, and he ducks behind the tree. He sticks his head out, and Cozzalio swings the minigun toward him and he ducks again. This game of "cat and mouse" is repeated several times.

Soon, the VC soldier behind the tree realizes that the minigun isn't working or is out of ammo. Ace sees him wave to the tree line to his rear and a group of Vietcong emerge, moving up to join him. Then the group of enemy soldiers starts slowly moving toward the Cobra. As they approach, the Vietcong combatants in the woods commence firing again.

As Munhofen hovers left to right in front of the Loaches, bullets can be heard pinging through the thin aluminum skin of the gunship. A couple of bullets hit the armor plating on the side of Bob's seat as he tries to get all his body behind the now seemingly small armored panel. Those few minutes seem like hours while Cozzalio and Munhofen anxiously wait for the Scouts to get loaded so they can lift out of there.

IT'S AN OLD WEST SHOOTOUT

The group of Vietcong continues their advance. Then Ace decides to take action. With his left hand, he swings his canopy upward, draws his .357-caliber revolver, and starts shooting over the nose of the Cobra.

Bob says, "Uhh, Ace, I think now they're gonna know we're out of ammo."

Cozzalio calmly replies, "Aw, it don't matter. We're gonna get our guys outta here any minute now." Ace's ploy works. The VC take cover each time he shoots, giving the Scouts precious seconds to load the downed Loach crew.

NEWKIRK'S PISTOL SHIELD

Back at the crash, Newkirk, restrained by the safety harness, is momentarily unconscious, hanging high in his seat. When he comes to, he looks out the busted windscreen and is peering down at the rice paddy mud. He struggles to get his lap belt released and cannot get it to open. Instinctively, he pulls the inertia release lever and falls forward, through the broken Plexiglas bubble, slicing his chin on the jagged plastic as he tumbles out of the aircraft into the rice paddy mud.

Slowly regaining his senses, he stands up and walks around the left side of the crashed Loach. In the distant tree line, he sees a multitude of muzzle flashes. Then, bullets hit the rice paddy at his feet, splashing mud in his face. "Oops, wrong way," he says to himself. He turns and goes around the other side of the Loach and sees Winsett, sitting in his OH-6 with his right arm outside the aircraft, motioning him to hurry and get in.

Arriving at Winsett's Loach, Newkirk climbs into the left side troop seat and fastens his safety harness. Winsett lifts the collective pitch control and carefully moves the cyclic forward. The heavily loaded Loach lifts off the ground and starts moving slowly forward. David reaches for his .45-caliber pistol, hoping to take revenge on the VC who shot him down. He fires one shot at the tree line and his pistol jams.

Note: Newkirk later finds that the AK-47 bullet that hit his pistol after grazing his knee lodged between the pistol grip and the magazine, preventing the .45-caliber cartridges from feeding into the chamber. Fortunately for David, his .45-caliber pistol, positioned between his legs, shielded him from a very painful bullet wound to a sensitive part of his anatomy.

DEPARTURE

Winsett's Loach slowly moves past the Cobra, gaining airspeed for liftoff. He takes off to the southeast while taking numerous hits on departure. "We can see the crap coming off their helicopter from the impacting rounds," said Munhofen. "They are getting shot up pretty bad. After the Loach goes by, the VC start picking on me and Ace again because we are still going slow, trying to pick up airspeed. They nail us pretty good too."

The two aircraft slowly gain airspeed and altitude. Together they limp back to Dong Tam.

Winsett lands at the 3rd Surgical Hospital helicopter pad and shuts down his Loach. Medics meet the helicopter, taking Newkirk inside to receive treatment for his injuries. He has a three-inch bullet crease on the inside of his right knee and a large gash on his chin.

After Newkirk is taken inside, Winsett tries to restart his Loach and finds it was so damaged by enemy fire that it is not flyable. It has two bullet holes in the engine, the instruments are blown out, part of the Plexiglas bubble is missing, and there are several holes in the rotor blades. The hospital staff demands that Gary move his Loach from the hospital's helicopter pad, but there is nothing he can do. Later, Maintenance arrives with a truck to haul the crippled OH-6 back to the airfield.

ROUND TWO

Munhofen and Cozzalio land at Dong Tam Airfield and shut down their aircraft. As soon as the rotor blades come to a stop, Cozzalio turns to Munhofen and says, "Come on, let's go. Let's get another aircraft. We've got to get back out there because the VC are going to take all the stuff off of that Loach."

They climb into another Cobra and head back to the area where Newkirk crashed. Bob and Ace fly over the rice paddy at five hundred feet expecting to find the Vietcong dismantling the aircraft. Instead, they are greeted with "baseball size" tracers from a .51-caliber antiaircraft gun. Evidently, the VC had time to set a trap.

"I dive for the deck," said Munhofen. "We start doing low-level, pop-up passes, unloading everything we have until we knock out the gun, and the bad guys just seem to disappear."

About a half hour later, three Lighthorse Slicks arrive to insert three fire teams of Doughboys to secure the crashed aircraft until it can be retrieved by helicopter sling load. Fortunately, the Vietcong didn't get the minigun, radios, or anything else from the downed Loach.

Back at the hospital, Newkirk's knee and chin are "stitched up" and bandaged. He returns to the Lighthorse troop area later that day.

Years later, Gary Winsett commented: "Munhofen and Ace performed the most heroic act of flying with no ammo. Newkirk and I were taking fire on the ground, and I could see the VC running in front of the bunkers. After they started their Cobra hover bluff, rounds quit hitting our Loach. Had they not intervened at the crash site, I doubt I would be here today."

Newkirk's Crash
David Newkirk and his crew chief survived this crash with no serious
injuries. This is an excellent example of the OH-6 crashworthiness.
Courtesy of David Newkirk

CHAPTER 22

LITTLE
RED-HAIRED GIRL

"Dreams are a vehicle for personal growth."

—ACE COZZALIO

ACE DISPLAYED GREAT CONFIDENCE AND determination. He could be flamboyant at times, but he was never cocky or boastful. Instead, he had the tenacity to succeed and a drive to excel that permeated everything he did. When with his flying buddies, he spoke with authority and held the attention of those around him.

Yet, in stark contrast to this "larger than life" persona, Ace was shy around women. He was soft-spoken and courteous, and his actions more closely resembled an eight-year-old boy approaching a girl at his first dance. This formality and politeness was acquired from his mother, Jan, who taught Ace to always be respectful toward women. This innocent shyness would soon be put to the task when Ace met the girl of his dreams.

DONUT DOLLIES

Other than nurses, most GIs served their tour in Vietnam without any contact with American women. The exception were the Donut Dollies, the affectionate name for members of the Red Cross Supplemental Recreational Activities Overseas (SRAO) program. To be a Donut Dolly, women had to meet the SRAO program qualifications, which included being single and a college graduate. Most were age 21 or 22. The program's goal was to boost the morale of U.S. combat troops in Vietnam, and many of these young women had been motivated to join by President John F. Kennedy's memorable call to "Ask not what your country can do for you—ask what you can do for your country." Wearing their easily identifiable powder blue dresses, the Donut Dollies were instructed to represent themselves to the soldiers as reminders of the girlfriends, wives, and sisters waiting back home.[19]

A unit of six Donut Dollies was stationed at Dong Tam. They were flown by helicopter to field locations throughout the Mekong Delta, where the 9th Infantry Division and Mobile Riverine Forces were operating. Once there, they entertained the troops with games and music and, at times, delivered a hot meal.

OH MY GOSH, WHO'S THAT?

Sherry Giles, a new Donut Dolly, arrives in Dong Tam in late January 1969. She is shown her room and given a brief orientation by fellow SRAO workers. Somewhere in the conversation, Tara, another of the Donut Dollies, says, "We usually go over to the Officers' Club in the evenings. Why don't you come join us?"

Later that evening, Sherry and Tara are sitting at a table in the O-Club talking with some infantry officers when they hear a commotion on the dance floor. Sherry turns and looks over her shoulder. On the dance floor are two tall guys doing a line dance with their sabers. "Oh my gosh, who's that?" asks Sherry. Tara replies, "That's Ace and Frank." A few minutes later the song ends. Cozzalio walks up and says, "Name's Ace. How ya doing?" He pauses briefly and says, "You're the little red-haired girl." Then he turns and walks off, leaving Sherry puzzled by what happened.

CHARLIE BROWN

Several weeks pass and Sherry settles into her the role of a Donut Dolly, traveling to field outposts throughout the Mekong Delta. One afternoon, an Army pilot arrives at the gate to the SRAO barracks where Sherry and the other Donut Dollies reside. One of the Donut Dollies approaches Sherry and says, "There's a guy at the gate. He says his name is Charlie Brown, and he wants to talk to the little red-haired girl. It must be you."

Sherry walks out to the gate and sees Ace. "Hi, I'm Charlie Brown," says Ace. "You're the little red-haired girl, and I have a peanut butter and jelly sandwich for you." In an imaginative reference to "Peanuts" in which Charlie Brown pines for the little red-haired girl while eating a peanut butter and jelly sandwich, Ace hands Sherry a small, paper-wrapped package. Sherry unfolds the paper to find two pieces of C-ration bread with peanut butter and jelly in between. This hard biscuit type bread is less than appetizing, even for the hungry GI in the field. Sherry is thinking to herself, "Eww, I'm not going to eat that." She thanks Ace for the gift, and he says, "Eat it," then waits expectantly. As Sherry tries to swallow the dry, unsavory concoction, she and Ace talk for a while, and then he leaves.

Several weeks pass before Sherry sees Ace again. She later learns he is on an assignment that takes him away from Dong Tam. When he returns, Sherry occasionally sees Ace at the O-Club, and he always stops to say hi.

In March, Cozzalio starts flying Cobra missions at night and has free time the following day. This gives him the opportunity to stop by and visit Sherry on the days she is scheduled to work in the unit office. It is through these visits that Ace and Sherry become close friends.

"Ace was different in the way he thought about things," said Sherry. "I found his conversations very interesting. He was a unique individual with very big dreams. Just talking with Ace, you knew he was going to pursue his dreams with every ounce of his seemingly boundless energy. And, he had lots of funny stories."

COBRA FLIGHT WITH SNEAKY SNAKE

When Ace started flying Cobra Gunships, his radio call sign was Crusader 36, with the numeral "6" denoting his role as gunship platoon leader. True to form, Ace decided he needed a unique name and came up with "Sneaky Snake." He used this call sign when making radio calls within the troop and took delight when his friends called him Sneaky Snake, or just "Snake."

One evening, Sherry told Ace about the Donut Dollies being transported in a 9th Aviation Battalion OH-6 to various field locations. On the return trip to Dong Tam, the pilot took the Loach up to ten thousand feet. She comments on how much fun it was flying in the Loach and going so high. Without saying a word, Ace mysteriously disappears. Minutes later, he returns with a flight suit and says, "Here, put this on."

Ace takes Sherry to the flight line, directing her to the revetment where his Cobra is parked. He opens the front canopy and assists Sherry in climbing into the copilot seat. He shows her the various controls and instruments and helps her don the flight helmet, plugging the commo cord into the microphone jack. He closes the canopy and goes to the other side to climb into the pilot's seat, behind Sherry.

Ace cranks the Cobra, brings it to a hover, and slides sideways away from the revetment. Then he makes a ninety-degree pedal turn and hovers to the runway. He calls the tower for takeoff clearance, and they lift off into the pitch-black Vietnam sky. It is a beautiful night. The sky is clear, and as the Cobra climbs to altitude, Sherry can see the sparkling village lights below and the twinkling stars above. "What a beautiful sight," she thinks to herself.

Ace flies north and tells Sherry they are going to land at Tan An. When they approach the airfield, he tells Sherry that she will make the radio call for landing clearance. Following Ace's instructions, Sherry keys the mic and announces, "Tan An Airfield, this is Sneaky Snake requesting clearance to land, runway two seven."

After a pause, a very excited voice responds, saying, "Roger that!" The tower operators were obviously surprised, and delighted, to be speaking to a female.

Ace lines up on the airfield and descends, coming to a hover over the runway. Then he tells Sherry she is going to experience the softest landing ever. He slowly sets the Cobra down, and she never feels the skids touch down. Ace is proud of his flying expertise and obviously pleased to "show off" for Sherry. Then Ace takes off and returns to Dong Tam.

The Cobra flight was totally unauthorized and a unique, rare experience for Sherry. Nothing was ever said about this flight, and only a few Lighthorse troopers knew it happened.

Ace and Sherry continued seeing each other when their schedules allowed. They would share stories and, in Sherry's words, "just be silly" at times, totally unlike the Ace that his flying buddies knew. Their friendship strengthened day by day. By the time Ace departed in June 1969, they were in love. They continued their relationship by writing letters until Sherry departed Vietnam in January 1970, and they were married in December 1970.

Ace and Sherry
Courtesy of Gary Winsett

CHAPTER 23

WARWAGON 16 IS DOWN

MOBILE RIVERINE MISSION - PLANNING MEETING

AT 1730 HOURS ON *FEBRUARY 24, 1969*, the Lighthorse Command & Control Huey lands on the USS *Benewah,* anchored in the Mekong River near Dong Tam. Major Brennon Swindell, D Troop commanding officer (Swindell assumed command of D Troop in December 1968), exits the helicopter and goes inside to meet with the 9th Infantry Division, 2nd Brigade commander and the S-3 Intelligence officer to discuss the following day's operation. Like previous missions, they review intelligence reports, study maps, and discuss plans for D Troop's reconnaissance support for the Mobile Riverine Force.

> Mobile Riverine Force (MRF)—The Mobile Riverine concept was first developed and practiced by the French navy, which preceded the Americans in Vietnam by more than a decade. Improving upon this concept, the modern MRF was a marriage of one U.S. Army infantry brigade and one specialized U.S. Navy task force. Together, the two units plied the waterways of the Mekong Delta searching for the elusive Vietcong.[20]

> In 1967, the U.S. Navy stationed the USS *Benewah* (APB—self-propelled barracks ship) and three other APB ships in

the Mekong River to support the 2nd Brigade of the 9th Infantry Division as a Mobile Riverine Force (MRF). Having a billeting capacity of nine hundred, the USS *Benewah* housed an infantry battalion and was essentially a self-contained amphibious assault force.

Using armored assault boats, the Navy landed the Mobile Riverine Force (typically one or two infantry companies) on the shore of the Mekong River. There, the infantry troops swept the area and attacked the enemy, with missions lasting several hours to several days. Later, the assault boats returned to a pick-up point to retrieve the MRF troops upon completion of their mission.[21]

The brigade commander details the mission. Early the following morning, two infantry companies of the Mobile Riverine Force will land on the south side of the Mekong River about ten klicks (six miles) downriver from Dong Tam, sweeping inland to the southwest.

Swindell receives orders to seek out and engage the enemy in an area southeast of Dong Tam near a geographical feature known as the "kitchen sink," because of the unusual appearance of the river. If Lighthorse encounters significant enemy activity, the MRF will revise their assault plan to land in the D Troop mission area instead. Likewise, if the MRF encounters enemy activity, Lighthorse will relocate to their area of operation.

As Swindell walks back to the C&C Huey, waiting on the ship's landing pad, he is confident D Troop will engage the enemy tomorrow. Intelligence reports show substantial enemy activity in this area, and while not officially labeled a "free-fire zone," Lighthorse and other aviation units have learned to suspect any activity in this area to be hostile.

Author's note: The following "Apparition" segment was taken from Ace Cozzalio's personal writings in which he described his experience the night preceding this mission.

THE APPARITION

Later that evening, Ace Cozzalio and Frank Bryan meet their fellow Lighthorse Troopers at the O-Club to drink a few beers, tell jokes, and listen to ever-enlarging war stories. After an evening of camaraderie with their friends, Ace turns to Frank and says, "Let's head for the hooch and get some shut-eye. We've got an early mission tomorrow."

Frank replies, "Yes, I'm beat. Let's hit the hay."

It is a hot, humid night as the two cavalry troopers return to their hooch, talking and joking along the way. In time, they are deep asleep on their army-issue cots. In the middle of the night, Ace is awakened by a weird, strangely cold sensation. He sits up in his cot and sees two ghostly images.

Ace asks, "Who are you?"

"Good morning, Mr. Cozzalio. My friend and I have been with you and Mr. Bryan for a long time."

"What do you want?" asks Ace.

"Well, Mr. Cozzalio, there are some problems that need to be discussed with you. Each person gets so many good luck chances in life, and you and Mr. Bryan have used up all of yours."

"What the hell are you talking about? Who are you?" asks Ace again.

"Our names are not important. Heed the words, 'Live by the gun, die by the gun.' So must it be."

As suddenly as they came they were gone, and the room was hot and stuffy again as Ace fell back asleep.

Later, Ace awakens to the ringing of his alarm clock. He reaches over to silence the alarm and lifts himself up to sit on the edge of his cot. He looks over at Frank, who is still sleeping soundly.

"Time to get up, Frank. Let's get moving," says Ace in a loud voice.

"Give me a break," says Frank.

"Listen to this, Frank. I had a far-out dream last night, that my number was up," says Ace.

"Not you, Ace, you are too damn mean," says Frank as he gets out of his cot and pulls on his jungle fatigue pants. "See you in OPS in twenty minutes."

THE RMF MISSION—FEBRUARY 25, 1969

At 0430 hours, Ace and Frank arrive at the Operations Center to receive the mission briefing. They find they are flying a search and destroy mission seven klicks (four miles) southeast of Dong Tam, an area familiar to both pilots. Previous missions in this area resulted in a shoot-out with the enemy. The terrain is heavily forested with nipa palm trees and dense vegetation, giving the enemy ample places to hide. Interspersed in between the forested areas are smaller open areas with low scrub brush and grass.

> Note: When Ace became Crusader Gunship platoon leader in early January 1969, Frank moved from Gunships to Scouts and became the Warwagon platoon leader with the call sign Warwagon 16.

Frank Bryan (L) and Gary Winsett (R) with a Warwagon Loach
Courtesy of Gary Winsett

At 0550 hours, the Cav Pack of two Warwagon Loaches, two Crusader Cobras, and the C&C Huey lift off from Dong Tam, heading southeast to their operations area. Frank is flying lead Scout in a Loach and Ace is flying lead Gunship in a Cobra. Swindell, the air mission commander, flying in the C&C Huey, monitors and controls the mission from above.

Arriving at the operations area shortly after sunrise, the two Scouts, with Frank in the lead, descend to fly low and slow over the trees, dropping to ground level when they come upon a clearing. They are searching for any sign of enemy activity. Occasionally, they circle back to check out a suspected hiding place, all the while enticing the enemy to fire and give away their position. High above, Ace and his wingman fly in a racetrack pattern. Cozzalio keeps his eyes focused on the location of Frank's Loach, ready to react quickly if the Scouts take fire.

The scouting continues for almost an hour, as they move from one sector to the next, searching for the enemy. Suddenly, as they swoop down across an open area, muzzle flashes are seen in the tree line to their left when the enemy opens fire on the Scouts. Frank calls, "taking fire, taking fire" while he and his wingman return fire, blasting the area with their miniguns and M-60 machine guns on their departure.

From high above, Ace immediately rolls into a diving gun run and calls, "Inbound, nails," firing flechette rockets into the woods as the Scouts move away. When Cozzalio breaks to climb, his wingman initiates a gun run to cover his departure. Ace and his wingman make several passes at the hostile area, firing 2.75-inch rockets, 7.62-millimeter minigun, and forty-millimeter grenades.

At some point, Swindell feels the enemy has been sufficiently pounded and calls the Cobras. "Crusader Three-Six, Lighthorse Six. Cease fire and return to altitude."

Then he calls the Scouts. "Warwagon One-Six, return to the AO for a battle assessment."

FRANK'S CRASH

The two Loaches fly in low and fast. When they approach the tree line where they previously took fire, Frank slows to look into the blasted vegetation. He makes one pass in front of the trees and sees no sign of the enemy. Then he circles left and returns to the tree line, only this time he lifts up and over the trees, following a footpath into the dense vegetation. Frank and his wingman continue flying at treetop level, maintaining about twenty to thirty knots (twenty-three to thirty-five mph) airspeed. Suddenly, Frank's Loach veers left in an erratic fashion, his rotor blades hitting a single dead tree trunk towering above the woods. The rotor blades separate and the Loach explodes as it falls into the dense vegetation.

From the air, Ace sees Frank crash and is stunned. He cannot believe what has happened. His best buddy went down in flames. Instinctively, he arcs the Cobra into a gun run. He calls, "Inbound," as he unleashes rocket after rocket into the trees near the crash. He feels helpless as he sees the Loach burning. The crash site is deep inside the forested area. There is no place to land. All he can do is place suppression fire around the crash site until ground troops arrive.

RECOVERY

Back at Dong Tam, the Doughboy Aero-Rifle Platoon is on stand-by, waiting near the Longknife Slicks staged along the runway. When Frank's Loach goes down, Swindell calls for the Doughboys, "Longknife Two-Six, Lighthorse Six. We have a Loach down. Repeat: Warwagon One-Six is down. Bring the Doughboys for rescue/recovery."

Longknife 26 turns to the troop and yells, "Mount up!" He raises his right arm in the air and, with his index finger circling, signals the pilots to crank their Hueys. The pilots and crew scramble to their aircraft. In seconds, turbine engines are whining and rotor blades are turning as the Doughboys grab their weapons and climb aboard. In ninety seconds, the three Hueys are at operating rpm, ready for takeoff.

In the lead Slick, Longknife 26 motions to Staff Sergeant Jim Flynn, the Doughboy Platoon sergeant. Flynn leans forward, and the pilot tells him, "Warwagon One-Six is down. We're going in to get them out."

As the three Hueys lift off and cross the Mekong River, Flynn spreads the word among the Doughboys in the Huey and silently hopes they get there in time for a rescue. After about seven minutes of flight time, the Longknife Hueys line up their approach to the open area adjacent to the tree line where Frank initially took fire. One by one the Hueys land and the Doughboys quickly exit the helicopters, taking defensive positions toward the tree line. As the Hueys depart, Flynn assembles the three fire teams, and they take the same path into the forest that Frank Bryan followed earlier.

The woods are dense with nipa palms and thick, tangled undergrowth. About sixty meters into the trees, they cross a stream. The path continues on the other side, and about a hundred meters further they find the crash. The Loach is still burning. The front of the aircraft is missing, and the bodies of both crewmembers are strapped in their seats. It is apparent that the white phosphorus grenades have exploded, either upon impact with the tree or set off by the fire. A Huey hovers above and drops two fire extinguishers to the Doughboys. With caution, they quickly extinguish the fire.

The Cav Team circles above, covering the Doughboys on the ground as they perform the unpleasant task of recovering the bodies of their fallen troopers. The mood is extremely dark. Everyone is asking why, why did this happen?

Eventually, the Doughboys return to the LZ and respectfully place two body bags aboard one of the Longknife Slicks. The three aircraft come to a hover and transition to forward flight as they lift off and rejoin the Cav Team for the return trip home.

Back at Dong Tam, the word has spread that they lost an aircrew. A large group of Lighthorse Troopers gathers at the flight line to await the arrival of the Cav Team. When the helicopters appear in the distance, there is an obvious missing aircraft in their formation—Warwagon 16. It is indeed a sad day for Lighthorse.

FRANK AND TOM REMEMBERED

Captain Frank Bryan and his crew chief, Specialist 4 Thomas Grose, perished in the crash. Everyone is impacted—Frank and Tom are two of the most popular troopers in Lighthorse.

The following day, D Troop has a solemn memorial service for their fallen troopers. Two cavalry sabers lie beside two white Cav hats resting atop yellow scarves on a table in front of the D Troop formation. After a dedication by Major Swindell, fourteen Lighthorse helicopters fly over the troop in the "missing man" formation. The flight is led by four Loaches with a missing spot in the right echelon of the V formation. Following are five Hueys and five Cobra gunships also in V formation. As the sound of helicopter rotor blades fades in the distance, "Taps" is played for Frank and Tom.

The cause of the crash is unknown. Since there was no radio communications prior to the crash, no one knows what happened. Later, Swindell, who observed the crash from above, said he believes Frank was shot, causing the aircraft to erratically swing left before impacting the tree.

Several days later, Captain Ace Cozzalio accompanies Captain Frank Bryan's remains back to Lynn, Alabama. Ace meets Frank's parents and presents them with the medals Frank was awarded while serving in Vietnam. After the conclusion of the funeral and graveside services, Ace returns to Frank's grave. He draws Frank's saber and, with a heavy thrust, plunges it point first into the ground. Then he ties a yellow scarf to the handle, gives a salute, and turns to walk away, forever regretting the loss of his best friend, Frank.

Later, in April 1969, Lighthorse names its newly constructed Troop Officers' Club "Frank's Fort" in honor of Frank Bryan.

Note: Frank Bryan's name can be located on panel 31W, Line 48 of the Vietnam Wall in Washington, D.C. Tom Grose's name can be found on panel 31W, Line 44.

CHAPTER 24

CAVALRY REVELRY

APRIL 1969

D TROOP IS INVITED TO the 9th Division Officers Mess in acknowl-
edgement of one of their more successful missions. For the cavalrymen, it is an honor and privilege to be invited to this prestigious
club. The Lighthorse troopers put on their best fatigue uniforms,
yellow scarves, white Cav hats, and sabers. True to form, Ace wears
his 1860s cavalry uniform complete with his silver belly Cav hat,
yellow scarf, riding boots, spurs, and saber.

Unlike the O-Club the cavalry troopers are accustomed to,
this Officers' Mess is very dignified with white tablecloths and
fancy glassware and silverware. The Lighthorse troopers arrive
en masse and pull several tables together to accommodate their
large group. After their meal and several drinks, the troopers
start singing Cav songs, becoming rather loud and boisterous
in a typical cavalry manner. To the casual observer, they most
likely think the D Troopers are rowdy and disorderly, but the
Lighthorse Officers feel they are properly subdued in this fancy
establishment.

Seated nearby, at another large table, is a group of infantry officers, dressed in their class B Khaki uniforms. The two
groups could not be more different, and that difference becomes increasingly apparent as the infantry officers also have
a few drinks.

Looking to their fellow soldiers at the other table, the infantry officers feel the D Troopers are having too much fun and don't show the proper decorum for a group of Army officers. And, they think the cavalrymen are arrogant and cavalier in their fancy uniforms.

Soon, competitive banter bounces back and forth between the two groups. This seemingly friendly exchange of insults and jokes continues for some time until a rather drunk infantry lieutenant stands up and boldly proclaims, "You pilots don't do a damned thing! All you guys do is fly around all day." Now this comment might have been passed over had the lieutenant not continued, "You don't get face-to-face with Charlie! Why, you don't even get dirty or sweaty up there in your air-conditioned helicopters!"

This comment hit a nerve with Ace. He stands, draws his saber, and raises it high above his head. The wide-eyed lieutenant takes a step backward as he looks at this tall cavalryman, dressed like someone out of a John Wayne movie. Ace chops the saber's blade down with a loud, resounding SMACK amid the glasses and dinnerware on the table between the two groups. The club becomes suddenly silent as Ace angrily shouts, "We do just as much [expletive deleted] gut fighting as you do, you son of a bitch!" He is ready and willing to take on the infantry.

Simultaneously, the Lighthorse Troopers and the infantry officers jump to their feet, each side taunting the other with deriding remarks. With approximately fifteen to twenty officers in each group, this standoff has the potential to become a nasty brawl. Then a couple of high-ranking officers come over and gently break it up, giving the officers an excuse to stand down with their egos in place.

Arriving at the conclusion that this "uppity place" is no fun, the D Troopers depart to their own Officers' Club and resume the party.

FRANK'S FORT

The D Troop O-Club is located in the Troop's well-built, heavily fortified bunker. Originally constructed to protect the troopers from the persistent VC mortar and rocket attacks, this building is constructed with double walls of stacked, heavy timbers with dirt packed into the twelve-inch void between the walls. The ceiling has ten- by sixteen-inch timbers running laterally with PSP runway planking laid on top of the timbers. Atop this is a standard A-frame roof with corrugated steel panels. Most likely, this is the best-built bunker on the Dong Tam complex.

Inside, the D Troopers decide to build their Officers' Club. They install wood paneling on the walls and hang appropriate cavalry posters and decorations. Then they construct a bar complete with refrigerator and an abundant supply of alcoholic beverages. The bunker is air-conditioned and becomes the "place to be" when under attack or ready to party. It is also a place to "decompress" after a trying mission, recall the day's activities, and play cards or other games.

Completed in April 1969, Frank's Fort quickly becomes known as the most popular "watering hole" in Dong Tam. Donut Dollies and several pilots from the B Company, 9th Aviation Battalion (Stingrays) frequently drop by to have a good time with the D Troopers. Like any decent club, the Fort has a massive stereo system, blasting popular music of the '60s. In addition to singing Cav songs, the troopers sing along with their favorite music. On any day, you might hear them singing "Respect" by Aretha Franklin or "We Gotta Get Out of This Place" by the Animals.

The Lighthorse pilots party long into the night, get a few hours of sleep, and, after their morning briefing, are on the flight line before sunup for the following day's mission. And, as one D Trooper aptly put it, "The fortunate ones get to do this over again the following day."

D TROOP CAV SONGS

She Wore a Yellow Ribbon

Around her leg
She wore a yellow ribbon,
She wore it in the springtime
And in the month of May,

And if you asked her why the hell she wore it,
She wore it for her lover in the 5th Cavalry.

Cavalry, Cavalry
She wore it for her lover
In the 5th Cavalry

To the Men of the Sword and the Yellow Cord
(From Ace's personal notes)

When troopers ride in column side by side
With destiny their only guide.
They care not what fate awaits them.
Prepared and loyal, death they do defy.
And so we'll drink this toast to the Cavalry.

Aye-eh-aye-eh-oh.

To the men of the dust and sabers thrust
I drink.

Aye-eh-aye-eh-aye-oh

The silent column marches proudly by
With horses heads held proudly high.
'Tis a picture that makes you certain,
The dear old Fifth shall never die.
So we'll drink this toast to the Cavalry.

Aye-eh-aye-eh-oh

To the men of the sword and the yellow cord
I drink.

Aye-eh-aye-eh-aye-oh.

CHAPTER 25

BATTLE ACROSS THE MEKONG

"Everyone is entitled to whatever success and achievement you
can realize through your own desire, capacity, and action."

—ACE COZZALIO

DONG TAM—MAY 1969

D TROOP HAD AN OUTSTANDING combat record in Vietnam. Lighthorse
pilots were dedicated, professional aviators. Through their com-
bat-proven tactics, they were highly effective in routing out and
destroying the enemy. And, in addition to the daily search and destroy missions, they were frequently called upon to "save the day"
when the 9th Infantry Division ground units were pinned down
or otherwise compromised by the enemy. Yet, no matter how well
they performed, there were always some high-ranking officers that
apparently did not appreciate the role of the air cavalry. They held
a certain distain for the cavalry troopers wearing their Stetsons
and scarves, feeling they didn't conform to their image of the "real
Army." It seemed these officers sought to make life difficult for the
air cavalry.

Such was the case in the 9th Infantry Division when an order
was issued that all aircraft attached to the division would display
the 9th Infantry Division "cookie insignia" (Octofoil design with red

over blue colors) on their aircraft. The addition of the insignia was not a problem; however, the order further specified that the "cookie insignia" must be placed on the upper aircraft cowling, near the rotor blades. This meant the Crusaders would have to remove their beloved Crusader shield from the Cobra gunship pylon inspection doors and replace it with the 9th Infantry Division insignia.

This directive infuriated the Gunship pilots. They were proud to be called Crusaders and likewise proud to display the Crusader emblem (shield with a red cross overlaying a sword) on their gunships. They felt that someone in the Division Staff had specifically targeted Lighthorse.

Ace Cozzalio, the Crusader platoon leader, was upset as well but followed through with the orders. Instead of painting over the existing pylon doors, he had the doors removed and replaced with new doors displaying the 9th Infantry Division insignia. Ace kept the "Crusader doors," waiting for an opportunity to implement a turnabout. That op-

Crusader Patch

portunity came shortly thereafter—and it was a big one.

WARWAGON 17 GOES DOWN—MAY 22, 1969

In the early morning daylight, a team of two Warwagon Scouts are flying low and slow over the terrain on the south side of the Mekong River about two miles downstream from Dong Tam. This area is heavily forested with dense vegetation, nipa palms, and banana trees. They peer into the tree line looking for any evidence of enemy activity. After several passes, it appears they are "skunked," unable to find anything of significance.

On this mission Warrant Officer Lorin Bliss is flying lead Scout with First Lieutenant Joe Duncan flying trail, off his right side. Bliss is an experienced Scout pilot, having flown Loaches for six months. He has a reputation for finding the Vietcong and attacking them head-on. For Duncan, this is his first mission as a Scout pilot, having flown as door gunner on two previous missions. Little does he know, he is about to receive his baptism in fire.

High above, two Cobra Gunships fly a racetrack pattern, constantly vigilant of the Loaches below. Captain Ace Cozzalio is flying Crusader lead with Warrant Officer Marty Tabor flying his trail. Ace sees an area that looks suspicious and calls Bliss. "Warwagon One-Seven, Sneaky Snake. Take a heading of zero seven zero and scout that area of nipa palms."

Lorin replies, "Roger that," and changes course to the northeast. As the Scouts approach the area, they start taking small arms fire from the tree line on their left. With guns blazing, they turn in the direction of the fire and take out two of the enemy combatants dressed in black pajamas with black and white checked scarves draped around their necks—Vietcong.

As they close on the woods, the two Loaches receive massive amounts of enemy fire from all along the tree line. Realizing they are outnumbered, the two aircraft swing to the right, taking evasive action.

"I am watching Lorin," says Duncan. "Little puffs of smoke and shit starts coming off his aircraft! Everybody's yelling, 'TAKING FIRE! TAKING FIRE!' My door gunner opens up with his M-60. I let go with the minigun." The two aircraft roll out of the turn and climb upward to fly above the woods.

Suddenly, Bliss' Loach starts losing power. He comes up on the radio and yells, "I'm gonna put this thing down!" No longer able to maintain altitude, the OH-6 starts descending.

"I see this little open area in front of Lorin," said Duncan. "He's on short final to it and I'm flying formation right behind him. He's about three feet off the ground, and a control rod or something must have snapped. His Loach noses over, hits the ground, and flips, end over end...BOOM...and catches fire. I see his crew chief scramble out the left side of the wreckage."

The crash site is hostile—in fact, the whole area is hot. The enemy is sporadically firing from the tree line along the perimeter of the open area. Lorin's crew chief takes cover near the crashed aircraft.

When Ace hears Lorin's call, he realizes Bliss is going down in a bad area. Seeing the disabled Loach crash, he immediately banks his Cobra to the left and dives toward the crash site.

Inside the crashed Loach, Lorin is momentarily dazed from the impact. As he gathers his senses, he realizes the aircraft is on fire, and he has to get out quickly. He is struggling to get the safety harness released when he looks up to see Ace's Cobra inbound, heading directly at him. "Seeing a Cobra come straight at you is something you never forget," said Bliss. Ace fires two rockets that hit in the woods in front of the crash, and a few seconds later two rockets hit behind the crash. "Ace was amazing," Bliss said later. "His ability to tuck his nose and put two ahead of us and two behind us saved our lives."

Duncan circles around and lands next to the crashed, burning Loach. There's still no sign of Bliss. Joe's crew chief jumps out and runs to the crash just as Bliss comes crawling out the other side. Lorin is disoriented. Thinking he hears someone call, he runs in that direction, away from the crash. Joe's crew chief runs after him, grabbing him and bringing him back to Duncan's Loach.

Meanwhile, Ace returns and hovers his Cobra high above the crash site, doing pedal turns, firing the minigun and forty-millimeter grenades into the perimeter of the open area while Bliss and his crew chief are loaded into Duncan's Loach.

Marty Tabor, in the trail Cobra, circles the area at two hundred feet altitude, also firing into the dense vegetation near the crash.

Duncan later commented, "There was Ace, hovering right above us. That crazy son of a bitch saved our butts."

With Bliss and his crew chief loaded in the passenger compartment, Duncan lifts off and heads back to Dong Tam. The crashed Loach continues to burn with a fire concentrated in the engine area.

Once Duncan's Loach has departed, Ace makes a final gun run, shooting a pair of "Willie Pete" (white phosphorus) rockets into the crashed Loach. It erupts in a brilliant white explosion, sending fingers of burning white phosphorus in all directions. This final act prohibits the Vietcong from acquiring the minigun and radios.

Duncan lands at the 3rd Surgical Hospital medical pad. Medics arrive and take Lorin and his crew chief inside for treatment. Then Joe lifts off and returns to the airfield, where he lands to assess his battle damage. He finds that his Loach is riddled with numerous hits from small arms fire. Duncan "lost his cherry" on his first day as a Warwagon Scout!

Meanwhile, the two Crusader Cobras return to Dong Tam to rearm and refuel. Ace is anxious to return to the fight. He wants to initiate contact before the Vietcong have time to move or regroup. He calls Operations and requests that another pair of Warwagon Scouts join the team on the flight line. Soon, the four aircraft are in the air headed back across the river.

Returning to the area where Lorin was shot down, they find the enemy has retreated into hiding. Even so, they discover hooches, bunkers, and military equipment hidden beneath the nipa palms, evidence of recent enemy activity.

SEND IN THE DOUGHBOYS

At this point, the size of the enemy force is unknown. It is estimated to be a small unit of VC, possibly a platoon or, at most, a company-size unit. Ace has a hunch that there is a larger force hidden in the dense forest, and he hopes to flush them out. He calls the air mission commander, requesting the Doughboys be inserted for a Reconnaissance in Force. The AMC agrees and calls Longknife 26, alerting him to launch the Slicks.

Anticipating this action, the Longknife Lift Platoon has been on standby at the Dong Tam Airfield. They immediately crank the three Hueys while three fire teams of Doughboys (eighteen troopers) climb aboard. In unison, the three Slicks take off and head across the river.

Meanwhile, the Warwagon Scouts are inspecting a landing zone in an open area about five hundred meters from the earlier crash. The LZ is U-shaped with the opening facing north, toward the Mekong River. It shows no signs of enemy activity and is about three hundred meters at its widest point, large enough for a flight of three Hueys to land in the middle with adequate distance to the wood line. The Scouts drop a yellow smoke grenade in the far end of the LZ and depart to the north.

After identifying the yellow smoke, the Longknives commence their approach from the river to the south. Once the Slicks are within two hundred meters of the LZ, the Crusader Gunships blast the tree lines on the western side of the LZ with rockets and grenades.

With door gunners firing their M-60 machine guns, the three Slicks continue their approach through the open end of the LZ and slow to settle in the clearing. The door gunners cease firing as the three Hueys touch down on the dry earth. As the aircraft's skids slide forward, coming to a halt, the Doughboys quickly exit both sides of the aircraft and move away from the helicopters. Then, in unison, the three Slicks come to a high hover, do a 180-degree pedal turn, and exit to the north across the river.

As the helicopters depart, the three fire teams of Doughboys promptly spread into assault lines to approach the woods about

150 meters to the west. The terrain is flat with waist-high grass and small shrubs. In line abreast formation, they cautiously advance toward the woods. As they close within fifty meters of the wood line, all Hell breaks loose. The Doughboys receive an enormous amount of enemy fire from the tree lines on the west and south sides of the LZ. In addition to AK-47 fire, a machine gun is firing from the woods to their front. The Doughboys immediately take cover and return fire. It is apparent they are vastly outnumbered. They call C&C and request an immediate "hot extraction."

In the meantime, a group of four Doughboys on the right flank evade enemy fire while advancing to the woods. Using the concealment of brush and undergrowth, they maneuver toward the machine gun. From a distance of about twenty-five meters, they hurl several hand grenades at the gun emplacement. The explosions create a flurry of activity in the woods around them. The enemy is moving and, fortunately for them, in the opposite direction.

This enemy activity is observed by the Warwagon Scouts, who together with Crusader Gunships attack the Vietcong when they emerge from the backside of the woods.

Sensing they have overextended their advance into bad guy territory, the four troopers quickly make their way back to the Doughboys in the LZ, where they take cover and wait for extraction.

Back at Dong Tam, the Longknife Slicks have just landed and shut down their engines when they received the call to return for the extraction. They immediately restart their engines and lift off, heading back across the Mekong River.

Once again, the three Hueys make their approach to the south while the Crusader Cobras fire rockets, miniguns, and grenades into the woods along the perimeter of the LZ. The Slicks land and the Doughboys scramble to load up. As before, they lift to a high hover, do a 180-degree pedal turn, and depart to the north. Fortunately, there are no casualties among the Aero-Rifle Platoon.

It was later determined that the Doughboys were unknowingly inserted into the midst of a large Vietcong encampment. This action is a precursor to a very large battle that lasts several days.

COBRA BATTLE: TWO-DAY SHOOT-'EM-UP

As the Longknife Hueys depart the LZ, on their return flight to Dong Tam, Cozzalio calls Lighthorse Operations. Realizing they are facing a substantial enemy force, Ace instructs OPS to launch all available Crusader Gunships. Of their nine Cobras, six aircraft are in flight status with one in maintenance and two held in reserve.

Warrant Officer Don Matthews has been in-country for two months, flying Cobras for the Crusader Gun Platoon. In recent weeks, he accumulated 160 flight hours and was grounded for a day or two to get his average flight time down. Don hears a commotion outside his hooch and goes out on the balcony to investigate. He sees several guys running toward the Operations Center. He hollers, "What's going on?" Someone yells back, "There's a big fight across the river. All Cobras are launching."

Don grabs his flight helmet, pistol, and gloves and heads for OPS. There he is paired with Warrant Officer Gary Callis as his copilot/gunner. Gary is a new guy who, after having a few beers, was heard to say, "I wanna get in a gun fight, I wanna get in a gun fight." Little did he know his wish was about to come true.

Together, Matthews and Callis rush to the flight line. They do a quick pre-flight inspection, climb into their crew seats, and crank their Cobra. Soon they are in the air, flying across the Mekong River. Arriving at the operations area, they see a single Cobra flying a racetrack pattern at 1,500 feet altitude. Ace Cozzalio, whose wingman recently departed to rearm at Dong Tam, is flying the gunship.

Matthews calls on the troop radio frequency, "Crusader Three-Eight, reporting for battle."

Ace replies, "Crusader Three-Eight, Sneaky Snake. Fall in behind me. We got some stuff going on, and I'm trying to get these guys to shoot at me."

Matthews takes the trail position behind Cozzalio. Shortly thereafter, Ace enters a diving gun run, firing rockets into the densely wooded area three klicks (two miles) south of the river.

Don tells Callis to get ready to shoot. Following Ace's lead, Matthews commences his gun run as Cozzalio breaks to climb. One after another, he fires pairs of rockets into the woods. Then Matthews hears that all-too-familiar plinking sound.

Gary says, "What's that?"

Don replies, "We're taking hits. Keep shooting."

The two Cobras circle around for the next run. Again, Don is in the trail position following Ace. When Cozzalio breaks off his gun run, Matthews commences his dive, unleashing rockets at the enemy concealed in the woods below. Suddenly, he takes a round through the canopy less than a foot in front of his head. Bits of Plexiglas hit his face, and he instinctively flinches from the "hits."

Don continues firing rockets and suddenly realizes it is strangely quiet in the front seat of the Cobra. He looks in the front mirror and can see Gary's face looking back at him. His eyes are wide open as he says, "Are you all right? Are you all right?"

Don replies, "Shoot! Shoot! These sons of bitches have zeroed in on us."

When they return to altitude, Don calls Ace, saying, "Sneaky Snake, Three-Eight. You may be trying to get them to shoot at ya, but they are hitting me."

Ace replies, "Roger that. Let's trade positions." On the next run, Matthews takes the lead with Cozzalio on his trail.

When the two gunships complete their diving assault and climb to altitude, four Cobras from D Troop join them. Now, there are six Crusader Gunships flying in a large racetrack pattern, diving at the wooded area and expending their ordinance on the enemy positions below.

The battle continues for several hours, and the word goes out for all gunships in the Dong Tam area to join the battle. Soon, five Cobras from the 9th Aviation Stingrays join the air assault. Now there are eleven Cobra gunships flying in a long daisy chain, each waiting their turn to blast the enemy with rockets, minigun, and grenades.

Typically, a Cobra gunship remains on station for two hours before returning to rearm and refuel. Today's action is so hot and heavy that the Cobras rearm three times before refueling. The Doughboys are called out to help man the rearming pads so the Crusader pilots can rearm without leaving the cockpit.

Landing on the rearming pad, the pilots bring their aircraft to flight idle while the Doughboys quickly arm them with 2.75-inch folding fin rockets, 7.62-millimeter minigun link ammo, and forty-millimeter grenade link ammo. Much like with a NASCAR pit crew, the rearming takes less than five minutes. Then the gunship lifts off to rejoin the fight across the river.

The air battle seems never-ending. Occasionally, the Army helicopters break off to allow the Air Force to join the fray, with Air Force fighter jets dropping 250-pound bombs. It is estimated that the Vietcong have a battalion-size unit directly across the river from Dong Tam.

This battle continues throughout the night and into the following day. Captain Bob Schultz, flying for the Stingrays, commented years later, "We were flying in a daisy chain nearly nonstop for several days. I remember not laying down in a bed for well over thirty-six hours. We just kept reloading and refueling, taking naps in the seat." (Note: Schultz later transferred to Lighthorse and flew Cobras for the Crusader Gun Platoon.)

Once the enemy forces are substantially battered by helicopter gunships, the 9th Infantry Division inserts two companies of 4th Battalion, 47th Infantry (Mobile Riverine Forces) into the area. The ground assault continues in the following chapter.

Prior to this incident, 9th Infantry Division Intelligence reports indicated there were no major concentrations of enemy forces in close proximity to Dong Tam. Small groups of Vietcong are known to be operating in the area, but there is no evidence of sizable forces. It is fortuitous that the Warwagon Scouts encountered the VC, and, through Ace's persistent probing, discovered the larger force hiding in the dense forest across the river. Had this Vietcong force not been discovered and eliminated, it is highly probable that the 9th Infantry Division would have been attacked at Dong Tam and suffered serious losses.

THE CRUSADER SHIELDS RETURN

At the conclusion of the battle, Cozzalio has the pylon doors with the 9th Infantry Division insignia removed from the D Troop Cobras and replaced with the Crusader shield doors. Ace made it known that the Crusaders had duly earned their identity, and he stood ready to defend his action to anyone who inquired. No one did. And, from that day on, the Crusader shields remain on the Cobras.

AH-1G Cobra Gunship
Courtesy of U.S. Army Aviation Museum via Ray Wilhite

CHAPTER 26

THE BATTLE CONTINUES

INFANTRY INSERTED—MAY 24, 1969

ON THE AFTERNOON FOLLOWING THE two-day Cobra shootout, C Company, 4th Battalion of the 47th Infantry (Mobile Riverine Force) is airlifted from the USS *Nueces*, their floating home on the Mekong River, to the previous day's battle area, three klicks (two miles) south of Dong Tam. Five Hueys, carrying the first sortie, line up on final approach to the landing zone. When the Slicks flare nose-up to slow their airspeed, they receive hostile fire from the tree line to the east. The Huey door gunners return fire with their M-60 machine guns as the Slicks settle into the LZ situated two hundred meters east of a dense coconut grove. When their skids touch down in the dry field with waist-high grasses, thirty soldiers promptly dismount, return fire, and establish a perimeter defense. The Hueys come to a brief hover, lift their tails, and take off with door gunners firing on their departure.

After the third sortie lands and drops the last group of infantry, three platoons (approximately ninety soldiers) assemble in line formation to advance toward the tree line. They move through the tall grass that eventually transitions to a rice paddy extending to the coconut grove. Upon entering the rice paddy, intense small arms fire erupts from multiple locations along the perimeter of the woods. The soldiers take cover and return fire.

Captain Dwight Beck, C Company commander, calls for artillery. The request is denied by Battalion Headquarters because another company is working the opposite side of the coconut grove. Beck is frustrated. His company is pinned down in the open rice paddy, and there is no way to advance on the enemy without artillery or air support.

CRUSADER COBRAS ARRIVE

Flying a support mission for the Mobile Riverine Forces, D Troop receives a call that C Company is under fire and needs gunship support. Several minutes later, Ace Cozzalio arrives in a Cobra gunship and places a radio call to Captain Beck. "Charlie Six, this is Crusader Three-Six with a flight of two gunships. How can I help ya today?"

Beck replies, "We've got bad guys in the tree line ahead of us. Can you take these guys out?"

Ace replies, "Roger that. We will be inbound shortly."

Cozzalio lines up on the tree line and makes a diving gun run from eight hundred feet altitude. Holding off on his rockets, he wants to get a better fix on the location of the bunkers. His copilot, in the front seat, swings the nose turret left and right, firing the minigun into the tree line. As they pass over the rice paddy in front of the tree line, Ace observes multiple bunkers in the forward edge of the coconut grove.

When Ace breaks to climb, Beck sees muzzle flashes and green tracer rounds emitting from the woods on the right flank of the departing Cobra. He calls Cozzalio and reports, "Crusader Three-Six, you have hostile fire from the wood line at your three o'clock."

"Roger that. We will hit them on our next run," replies Ace. Cozzalio circles around and lines up for another gun run.

At the moment the Cobra initiates its dive, Becks sees a VC soldier emerge and stand on top of a bunker. He shoulders an

AK-47, takes aim, and starts firing at Cozzalio's gunship. Beck calls, "Crusader Three-Six, you have a Victor Charlie on top of that bunker firing at you."

Ace replies, "Roger that. I got him in my sights." Cozzalio continues his dive as the gutsy VC takes a stand, firing directly at the gunship diving toward him. It is a face-to-face standoff—although the gunship has a considerable advantage. Then two HE (High Explosive) rockets streak from the Cobra toward the bunker.

Beck said later, "There was a big explosion, and both the VC and the bunker were disintegrated."

As Cozzalio breaks to climb, he calls Beck. "Charlie Six, there are many bunkers in the edge of the woods. We'll keep working them for ya."

Ace and his wingman make repeated gun runs on the tree line, attacking one bunker after another. The Vietcong stand their ground and vigorously defend their fighting positions. Green tracers erupt from the woods, streaking in the direction of the Cobras each time they break to climb after completing their gun run.

Meanwhile, the three platoons attempt to maneuver closer to the wood line. Using a drainage gully, the platoon on the left flank maneuvers to within fifteen meters from the tree line, unable to go farther because of intense enemy fire and the rocket explosions in the woods. The other platoons move from one rice paddy dike to the other and eventually take cover in the middle of the rice paddy, about seventy-five meters from the tree line.

After an hour of repeated gun runs on the bunkers, Cozzalio calls Beck, saying, "Charlie six, Crusader Three-Six. We gotta leave now to rearm and refuel. We'll be back soon."

Beck replies, "Roger that. We sure appreciate you guys."

After landing at the Dong Tam rearming pad, Ace and his wingman do a quick damage assessment and discover that their aircraft have many bullet holes from small arms fire. Noticing that his wingman seems concerned, Ace says, "Hey man, it's no problem. It's all in a day's work."

Approximately thirty minutes later, Ace and his wingman return to the AO and continue attacking the bunkers. This battle continues until dusk approaches, and the Crusader Cobras must return to home base.

Ace calls Beck and says, "Charlie six, our job is done here. We are headed home. Good luck chasing Charlie." Then the two Cobras bank left and return to Dong Tam.

INFANTRY SWEEPS THE AREA

With nightfall approaching, C Company pulls back and consolidates into a defensive position adjacent to the coconut grove. On the following morning, they advance into the woods and discover ten to fifteen bunkers, most of which have been destroyed by the Cobra airstrikes. There are many blood trails but no bodies in the bunkers. Evidently the Vietcong withdrew during the night, taking their dead and wounded with them.

They continue sweeping east through the coconut grove while A Company sweeps west from the other side. They discover a hospital, a maintenance facility, and massive amounts of weapons and equipment concealed in the densely wooded areas. They also find many dead from the previous days' Cobra battle.

At the completion of their mission, the infantry companies report ninety-two KBAs (Killed by Attack).[22] Documents discovered in the battle area indicate they were fighting the 516th Vietcong Main Force Battalion.[23]

Later, Captain Beck commented on the mission. "The Cobra air strikes were right on the money. Precision was important because our left flank was so close to the enemy bunkers that we could hear the shrapnel flying overhead when the rockets exploded. Had it not been for the Cobras that day, it would have been a bloody afternoon for C Company."

For his action that day, Ace is awarded the Distinguished Flying Cross (his fourth award). The award document states, "With complete self-disregard, Captain Cozzalio continued exposing himself to enemy fire until the bunker complex was silenced."

Ace Flying Cobra Gunship
Courtesy of Rex Cozzalio

CHAPTER 27

MOTHER HEN

SAVING THE BEST FOR LAST, the next two chapters are a slight step backward in the chronological sequence of events. Both incidents occurred on January 25, 1969, three weeks after Ace assumed command of the Crusader Gunship platoon and two days before being promoted to captain.

Little did he know at the time, but Ace's courageous actions on this day would be recounted time and time again by his fellow cavalry troopers and the infantry soldiers on the ground who only knew him as that "crazy helicopter pilot."

LRRPs Locate NVA—North of Phu My Village

At 1045 hours, a seven-man LRRP team from E Company, 50th Infantry (the 9th Infantry Division's Long Range Reconnaissance Company) grabs their gear and boards a single Huey helicopter sitting on the small pad at Tan An—the 3rd Infantry Brigade's base camp. Their mission is to follow up on intel reports of enemy activity in a wood line twelve klicks (seven miles) west of Tan An in the Plain of Reeds. Expecting a quick reconnaissance mission lasting no longer that three or four hours, the team packs light—weapons, radios, and LBEs (web belt and suspenders carrying canteen and ammo pouches), forgoing the heavy rucksacks carried on longer missions.

As the Huey lifts off in a westerly direction, the LRRP team leader, Sergeant Jim Thayer, wearing tiger-stripe camo fatigues, camo face paint, and a headband, turns to observe his team. He glances momentarily at each team member, locking eyes, giving assurance that everything is going as planned. Four of his team are wearing standard-issue camo fatigues and boonie hats and likewise have camo face paint. Two of the team are PRUs, who like Thayer are wearing tiger-stripe camo fatigues and camo face paint. Having been with the PRUs on previous outings, Thayer has great confidence in their combat skills and loyalty.

PRU—Provisional Reconnaissance Unit: Small teams of tough Vietnamese paramilitaries used to seek out and eliminate the Vietcong. Most were highly experienced combat veterans who survived many years in elite combat units before coming to the PRU. All of them had a deep hatred for the VC, primarily because of atrocities committed against them and their families.[24] Oftentimes, one or two PRUs were assigned to LRRP teams.

Nearing the operations area, the Huey makes a rapid descent from altitude and levels out at thirty feet AGL, flying fast and low across the open countryside. Seated in the open cargo doors with their legs dangling outside the aircraft, the LRRP team, with weapons in one hand, holding on with the other hand, get ready to exit the Slick.

Moments later, the Huey flares to slow its approach and each of the LRRPs repositions to stand on the aircraft's skids. As the Slick settles downward through the last three to four feet AGL, the team members jump off. Feeling the aircraft suddenly go light, the pilot hears his crew chief say, "We're up." He immediately pushes the cyclic forward and pulls in power with the collective. The Huey's tail lifts high in the air as the aircraft makes a rapid departure.

The LRRP team quickly deploys and takes cover behind a long berm of earth, about three to four feet high. Thayer's eyes scan the surrounding terrain as he makes a quick appraisal of their situation. They are fifty meters southwest of a wood line bordering the Rách Lang Cát Canal. The grass is knee high and there is no cover between their position and the woods. Their only course of action is to cross the open area toward the trees, hoping to reach the wood line before being detected. On Thayer's signal, they promptly assemble in patrol formation and move out in the direction of the woods with one of the PRUs taking point (lead) and the other taking drag (trail) positions.

THE WOODS ERUPT WITH GUNFIRE

Just prior to reaching the trees, the point PRU senses something and turns left, walking parallel to the tree line, cautiously inspecting the wooded area before entering. Suddenly, an NVA soldier, dressed in khaki uniform and olive/gray NVA web gear, stands and aims his AK-47 at the point man. Sergeant Thayer, in spot two position, fires his M-14 rifle and drops the NVA from a distance of about ten feet. At that moment, a massive amount of small arms fire erupts from inside the woods. At least a platoon of NVA soldiers opens fire on the LRRP team from less than fifteen meters away.

Some of the team drops to one knee to fire while others are moving left to right to keep the enemy from drawing a bead on them. The team is essentially caught in the open near the edge of the woods with nothing behind them but wide-open terrain and no place to take cover. In an instant the battle is raging all along the tree line.

Out of the corner of his eye, Thayer sees Specialist 4 Mike O'Day take off running to the right chasing after a NVA soldier wearing a pith helmet who is scrambling along the edge of the woods. O'Day stops, shoulders his rifle, and puts a single round through the back of the soldier's neck, tumbling him into the heavy cover.

Then Thayer sees something incredible. On the left side, the two PRUs are standing in the open about ten meters from the wood line in a heated exchange with the NVA soldiers hidden in the trees—alternately firing their rifles and shouting in Vietnamese back and forth. Interspersed in the rapid-fire language and gunfire is an occasional obscenity spoken in English and evidently understood by both adversaries. Months later, Thayer learned that the NVA were trying to convince the PRUs to turn on their American comrades and kill them—promising to spare the PRUs if they did so. This tactic, however, only served to increase the PRUs' resolve to fight.

RTO Is Down

The RTO, Specialist 4 Richard Bellwood, is on the radio behind and to the left of Thayer. He hollers to Jim, "What do you want me to do?" Thayer replies, "Shoot." Bellwood drops the radio handset and starts shooting his M-16 at the NVA in the wood line. Moments later, a round hits Bellwood in the right hip. As he falls to the ground, he yells, "Jim!"

Thayer turns to see Bellwood on the ground in severe pain. He runs to his side and, on one knee, he cradles Bellwood's neck in the crook of his left arm. At that moment, an NVA soldier stands and opens up with an AK-47 on full automatic. Two rounds hit Bellwood in the chest, knocking him unconscious. One round hits Thayer in the right shoulder and another hits the canteen on his web belt.

Thayer drops and rolls to the right, away from Bellwood. He comes up firing from the hip and hits the NVA soldier who had shot him and Bellwood. The man staggers and drops backwards into the underbrush. Jim realizes he must call for air support, and Bellwood's radio just took two AK-47 rounds. Crawling to the right, along the edge of the trees, Thayer searches for the rest of his team. Seeking the junior RTO, he yells, "Laurer," who replies, "Here." He low-crawls to Specialist 4 Steve Laurer and finds Laurer, also wounded, on his feet, moving and shooting.

Taking the handset from Laurer, Thayer uses the radio to call for artillery or gunship support after learning that Laurer had already reported their engagement with the NVA. He calls the E Company, 50th Infantry relay team at Tan An, telling them, "We've got gooks everywhere. They are all over the damn place. At least a platoon, probably a company of NVA regulars."

The relay team tells Thayer that gunship support is on the way. Then the relay team calls 3rd Brigade Headquarters (also located at Tan An), reporting the LRRP's engagement with an estimated company-size unit of NVA soldiers.

ACE TO THE RESCUE

Seconds later, two Cobra gunships from D Troop, 3-5 Air Cavalry arrive over the embattled LRRP team. From the air, Crusader lead Ace Cozzalio can see the team scattered over the open terrain ten to fifteen meters from the tree line. It is obvious that the LRRPs are fighting for their lives.

Cozzalio calls on the LRRP radio frequency and asks, "Tango One-One, this is Crusader Three-Six with two Cobra gunships. How can we help?"

Thayer replies, "Hit anything in the woods."

Ace replies, "You got it."

At that instant, Cozzalio banks his gunship sharply left, making a descending turn over the open area to the rear of the LRRPs. Leveling off at thirty feet altitude, he returns flying directly toward the LRRPs' position. Coming to an abrupt hover above and behind the embattled patrol, the gunship hangs boldly in the air, like a protective mother hen. Doing pedal turns left and right, Ace blasts the trees with rockets, miniguns, and forty-millimeter grenades. Amazingly, the NVA stand their ground and continue to return fire at the hovering Cobra. Meanwhile, Cozzalio's wingman makes a wide circle around the LRRPs at two hundred feet altitude, also firing into the tree line.

Beneath the battling Cobra gunship, the LRRPs continue to fire into the woods. Due to his shoulder wound, Thayer fires his M-14 from the hip and goes through two magazines of ammo. Then he hears the familiar *Wop, Wop, Wop, Wop, Wop* of an approaching Huey.

The helicopter approaches low from the south and flares to land about thirty meters behind the LRRPs, with its right-side open cargo door facing the tree line. When the Huey touches down, Ace does a pedal turn to the left and lifts off in a westerly direction, joining his wingman, circling overhead. There, the two gunships continue firing into the woods in front of the LRRPs to cover their extraction.

Two LRRP team members grab Bellwood under each arm and drag him to the waiting helicopter as the door gunner provides cover fire with the Huey's M-60 machine gun. Once Bellwood is loaded, Thayer shouts, "Mount up!" and the four remaining team members scramble toward the Huey. Thayer is last to climb aboard as the helicopter gets light on its skids. Then the Huey lifts off and departs to the southwest, taking the wounded LRRPs to the medical aid station at Tan An. Once in the air, Thayer realizes that four of his seven-man LRRP team are wounded including Specialist 4 Richard Bellwood, whose life is hanging in the balance. Seeing that Bellwood needs prompt medical attention, Thayer yells at the pilots to hurry.

After the Huey departs, Cozzalio and his wingman join up with the D Troop Cav Team and return to Tan An to rearm and refuel. That afternoon, the Cav Team resumes its search and destroy mission in the area west of Tan An.

Medevac

When the Huey touches down on the medical pad at Tan An, a half dozen medics rush to the helicopter and promptly place Bellwood on a gurney and wheel him into triage. The other wounded LRRPs follow closely behind. Inside, Bellwood is wheeled into the operating room where a team of doctors starts working on him.

After wrapping Thayer's shoulder to stop the bleeding, the medic tells him the bullet left no exit wound and lodged somewhere in his back. He has to be medevaced to the Tan Son Nhut hospital in Saigon to have the bullet surgically removed. About that time, one of the doctors working on Bellwood approaches Thayer and says, "He's gone. There's nothing else we can do." Thayer is absolutely devastated. Richard Bellwood was like a kid brother to Jim.

Shortly thereafter, Thayer is loaded on a Dustoff Huey helicopter and medevaced to Saigon for surgery. After recovering from surgery, he is greeted by Major General Julian Ewell, 9th Infantry Division commanding officer, and Captain Dale Dickey, Jim's company commander. In a brief casual ceremony, General Ewell presents Thayer with the Silver Star and Purple Heart. Then, he informs Thayer that he is promoted to Staff Sergeant—a complete surprise. Thayer is flown to Camp Zama, Japan, where he recovers for nine weeks before returning to his unit.

As a result of the LRRP mission, Specialist 4 Richard Bellwood is posthumously awarded the Silver Star. Specialists 4 Mike O'Day and Steve Lauer are both promoted to sergeant and also receive Silver Stars. Specialist 4 Willy Boone receives the Bronze Star with V device for valor.[25]

Years later, Jim Thayer commented, "We were about to be overrun by the NVA. The Cobra gunships arrived in the nick of time to save our butts. Had they not arrived when they did, I would not be here today."

THIS IS JUST THE BEGINNING

For Ace Cozzalio, this is just the start of an extraordinary day. He encounters even more action later that afternoon and his flying feats are even more astonishing.

CHAPTER 28

ACE DESTROYS THE BUNKER

THE LRRP'S DISCOVERY OF A large-scale unit of NVA regulars operating near Tan An is viewed as significant intelligence. The 9th
Infantry Division command group springs into action, realizing
this is an opportunity to strike quickly before the enemy forces
have time to relocate. The hostilities that develop that afternoon
result in one of the major 9th Infantry Division battles in 1969—
the Battle of Phu My.

In the initial engagement, an infantry company of ninety soldiers is pinned down by an NVA machine gun in a hidden, fortified bunker. Once again, Ace Cozzalio arrives to save the day. In
this unusual occurrence, we see Ace relinquish his Gunship pilot duties to resume his previous role as an aggressive Scout pilot.
What follows is a firsthand account of this story from the perspective of both the infantry soldiers on the ground and the cavalry
pilots in the air.

THE BATTLE OF PHU MY

The 3rd Brigade commander sees an opportunity to surround
the NVA by launching a large-scale airmobile operation, inserting
five infantry companies around the perimeter of the NVA location. Two companies of the 5th Battalion, 60th Infantry and three

companies of the 2nd Battalion, 60th Infantry are alerted to assemble and make ready for helicopter insertion.[26]

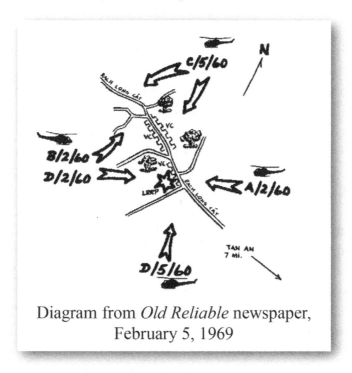

Diagram from *Old Reliable* newspaper,
February 5, 1969

CHARLIE COMPANY—RACH KIEN BASE CAMP

C Company, 5th Battalion, 60th Infantry is notified they are the first company to be inserted along a canal north of Phu My village, where the LRRP team engaged the NVA. The acting company commander, First Lieutenant Roger Vickers, meets with his two platoon leaders and First Lieutenant Hugh Best, an artillery forward observer, who is joining them to coordinate artillery fire support. Vickers tells 3rd Platoon that they will be the first unit on the ground, followed by 1st Platoon and then 2nd Platoon. Vickers, his two RTOs, and Best will join 3rd Platoon in the first helicopter sortie. Vickers' decision to accompany the lead platoon is likely influenced by the absence of the 3rd Platoon leader that day.

Note: Charlie Company has a proud history. In World War II, they fiercely attacked German bunkers on Omaha Beach. Afterward, captured German intelligence reports stated that this unit fought so valiantly that they were surely a Ranger Company. From that day on, they were nicknamed "Charlie Rangers." Originally designated 1st Battalion, 16th Infantry of the 1st Infantry Division, the 1st Battalion swapped colors with 5th Battalion, 60th Infantry of the 9th Infantry Division in September 1968.

The platoon leaders alert their men to grab their gear and assemble for a mission. The troops are quick to ask, "Where are we headed?" When they hear the response, "Plain of Reeds," the mood turns somber. Charlie Company has journeyed into the Plain of Reeds on many missions. The terrain is unforgiving and, most often, enemy contact results in casualties.

An aviation company of five D Model Huey helicopters is assigned to transport Charlie Company to the operations area. Carrying five or six soldiers and gear, each sortie of five Slicks carries a platoon. It will take three sorties to transport the entire company, with a thirty- to forty-minute interval between sorties.

Assembling in groups of five or six soldiers alongside the road outside their base camp, 3rd Platoon waits the arrival of the Hueys. Vickers, his two RTOs, Best, and his RTO are there as well. It is a typical day in the Mekong—hot and humid. The sky is clear and the wind is calm, barely enough breeze to disturb the leaves on the nearby nipa palms.

Soon the Charlie Rangers hear a familiar *Wop, Wop, Wop, Wop, Wop* sound, and five Huey helicopters appear over the trees in the distance. Seconds later, they descend and set down on the road.

The soldiers grab their gear and quickly load through the open cargo doors on both sides of the Hueys. In unison, the five Slicks come to a hover and take off in a westerly direction.

Note: The company commander is accompanied by two RTOs carrying PRC-25 backpack radios with three-foot whip antennas. The senior RTO carries the Battalion Command Radio to communicate with the Battalion Tactical Operations Center. The junior RTO carries the Company Radio to communicate with the platoons, squads, and Charlie Company Operations at the Rach Kien base camp. The whip antennas are easy to identify and make the RTO and others near him (most likely the commander) a primary target for enemy fire.

Approximately fifteen minutes later, the flight of five Hueys arrives in the operations area. After scouting the location, an OH-6 helicopter drops a colored smoke grenade to mark the landing zone, two hundred meters northeast of the wood line. The flight leader identifies the smoke color, and moments later starts a gradual descent toward the landing zone. Following close behind, each of the Hueys commences its descent while stacked a little higher than the aircraft in front of it. Approximately three hundred meters from the LZ, the Huey door gunners start firing their M-60 machine guns to suppress any enemy combatants that might be lurking in the nearby woods.

One by one, the five Slicks flare to slow and settle into the landing zone. When the aircraft skids touch the ground, the door gunners cease firing and the 3rd Platoon soldiers quickly exit both sides of the Hueys, taking cover away from the aircraft.

Like most areas in the Plain of Reeds, the landing zone is covered with tall grasses and reeds ranging in height from waist to chest high. This is the dry season. What previously was knee-deep water and mud is now parched and cracked dirt.

The Hueys depart to the south with door gunners firing M-60 machine guns *rat-tat-tat-tat-tat-tat*. As the sound of the helicopters fade in the distance, the platoon quickly assembles and forms up in column formation with 2nd Squad in the lead, Vickers and the Command Group next, followed by 1st Squad. They move out in the direction of the woods bordering the open area. The point man, Specialist 4 Jerry Lemons, leads the column toward the wood line. Unlike the straight and narrow tree lines that border rice paddies elsewhere in the Delta, this wooded area has an irregular perimeter jutting in and out of grassy open area.

Unbeknownst to the Charlie Rangers, a concentrated force of NVA soldiers is concealed inside the perimeter of the wood line at ten- to twenty-meter intervals. Yet, despite the hidden danger all along the tree line, an even greater peril lies waiting in the woods. Directly in front and slightly to the left of the advancing column, an enemy machine gun bunker is positioned near the edge of the tree line. This large fortified bunker is dug into the ground about four feet deep, providing an interior area accommodating up to four soldiers. The sides consist of packed dirt and dried, hardened mud, creating an enclosure that is impervious to small arms fire. The structure protrudes out of the ground about thirty inches high with a roof constructed of six- to ten-inch diameter timbers covered with dirt. The bunker is roughly ten feet wide with a twelve- to fourteen-inch open gun port running across the front. On the backside, a small entryway is barely large enough for two soldiers to pass through. The entire bunker is camouflaged with brush and grass, making it very difficult to detect.

Inside, the NVA soldiers are manning a Chi-Com PKM 7.62-millimeter belt-fed machine gun with a practical firing rate of 250 rounds per minute and a range of one thousand meters. They also have several AK-47 rifles. From their camouflaged and well-hidden position, the enemy gunners have a field of fire covering almost the entire open area. The NVA soldiers remain perfectly quiet and hidden, patiently watching the Americans advance. Charlie Company is walking directly into a deadly trap.

THIRD PLATOON IS AMBUSHED

As they make their way through the tall grass, the Charlie Rangers pass two dead NVA soldiers, killed earlier by artillery or gunship barrages. This discovery serves to heighten the tension— the troops realize the enemy is nearby.

When Lemons gets within twenty meters of the woods, three NVA soldiers emerge on their left and take off running along the edge of the tree line. Vickers hollers, "Second Squad, go after them." With Lemons in the lead, Second Squad takes off running ninety degrees from the column. After chasing the enemy about seventy meters, Lemons stops, shoulders his M-16, and shoots one of the NVA soldiers in the back, killing him instantly.

Meanwhile, Vickers and the command group, now at the head of the column, continue moving toward the woods. They enter the perimeter of the irregular tree line about the same time that Lemons fires his M-16. At that moment, the entire wood line explodes with AK-47 and machine gun fire. The troops hit the ground, taking cover and returning fire. Some hide behind small mounds of dirt, but most are caught in the open, seeking cover in the tall grass.

The command group and 1st Squad of 3rd Platoon are within ten to twenty meters of the machine gun in the well-hidden bunker slightly to their left. At this close range, the group is an easy target for the enemy gunner, and they encounter most of the initial casualties.

All along the wood line, intense enemy fire from the NVA fighting positions has the Americans pinned down, unable to maneuver or retreat. The tall grass makes it difficult to determine where the enemy is located. Every time they raise up to look, they attract an onslaught of enemy fire.

On the left flank, Lemons and Private First Class Albert Gulliver dive for cover behind a small earthen dike that is barely high enough to shield their bodies. They are ten meters from the tree line and can see NVA soldiers shooting and maneuvering inside the woods. Lemons engages a fighting position to his left while Gulliver repeatedly fires his M-79 grenade launcher into the moving groups of enemy soldiers in the woods.

THE CO IS KILLED

The commanding officer, Vickers, is suddenly cut down by massive enemy fire from the machine gun in the bunker. His junior RTO, Specialist 4 Dennis Holzheimer, lay dead beside him. Hugh Best, the artillery forward observer, is seriously incapacitated with a chest wound. In a matter of seconds, three of Charlie Company's five-man command group are killed or incapacitated.

Following behind the command group, 1st squad leader Sergeant James Riggins is killed by the machine gun fire from the bunker. And, before he can return fire, the squad's machine gunner, Corporal Jay Rumsey, is also killed.

Standing next to Vickers, the senior RTO, Specialist 4 Norman Prance, hits the ground, taking cover in the tall grass about ten meters from the enemy bunker. Prance, an experienced RTO, is quick to assess the dire situation. He realizes the NVA gunner can detect any movement of the grass. He lies motionless as he calmly places a radio call to 5th Battalion Tactical Operations Center, advising them of the situation and requesting support.[27]

1ST PLATOON INSERTED

Ten to fifteen minutes later, the second sortie of five Hueys arrives carrying 1st platoon, commanded by First Lieutenant John Depko. While flying inbound, the flight leader receives a radio call advising that 3rd Platoon is taking fire and the landing zone is hot. He, in turn, calls his flight, announcing they are flying into a hot LZ and will come in low with suppression fire inbound. Then the flight leader turns to Depko. He reaches up and moves his helmet microphone away from his mouth and yells, "You have a hot LZ." Depko nods and turns to spread the word among his troops.

The five Slicks make their approach low and fast. As they close on the landing zone, the door gunners open up with their M-60 machine guns, firing into the wood line. In unison, the five aircraft flare to slow and touch down in the tall grass about a hundred meters behind 3rd Platoon. The Huey door gunners cease firing and the five groups of infantry soldiers dismount quickly, taking cover in the high grass. The Hueys come to a momentary hover, lift their tails, and fly low across the open area on their exit to the southeast with the door gunners firing again.

After the Slicks depart, there is a strange silence as 1st Platoon forms in line formation to advance upon the tree line. On Depko's command, they cautiously move toward the woods. After advancing about twenty meters, an explosion goes off near the tree line to their front and AK-47 fire rips through the tall reeds. The soldiers hit the ground seeking cover. More explosions. Wounded men to their front are screaming for medics. The tall reeds and grasses block their view, yet provide some element of cover. Confusion reigns. Realizing that 3rd Platoon is pinned down somewhere to their front, 1st Platoon is cautious not to fire in that direction. After assessing the situation, Depko calls out firing instructions to his men. "Return fire, ten o'clock. Return fire, ten o'clock."

In response to the calls for help, Specialist 4 James Luckey, 1st Platoon's medic, low crawls forward to 3rd Platoon. Sometime later, arriving in the area of the downed command group, his movement is detected by the machine gunner in the bunker, and he too is killed.

2ND PLATOON ARRIVES

With a thirty-minute turnaround, the third sortie of five Slicks returns with 2nd Platoon, commanded by First Lieutenant Duane Anders. Once again, the five Hueys come in low and flare to settle into the LZ on the right side of 1st Platoon. The soldiers quickly jump out of both sides of the helicopter, taking cover. The five Hueys lift off and depart to the south.

Moments later, Anders gets a radio call from Battalion informing him that the company commander has been killed and he is now in command. At this point, 3rd Platoon is pinned down directly in front of the machine gun bunker. First Platoon is pinned down fifty to seventy meters behind them, and 2nd Platoon is positioned on the right side of 1st Platoon, about a hundred meters from the tree line. Anders realizes he needs to maneuver his platoon forward to the wood line in an effort to flank the machine gun bunker.

The grass in this area is sparse, providing little cover for the Charlie Rangers. Anders orders his platoon to advance toward the woods using squad movement, a time-honored infantry technique of alternating one squad providing cover fire while another squad is moving. The squads leapfrog across the open area to the wood line. At the very moment they enter the woods, the machine gun in the bunker opens up and pins them down.

The platoon medic, Specialist 4 Albert Guillorn, said, "I saw puffs of dirt kicked up where the bullets were hitting the ground around us. I hit the ground seeking cover, but the grass in this area was too short. I was exposed. Up ahead I can see a rock about three feet in diameter. I low crawl about ten feet to the rock and take cover just as bullets ricochet off the other side."

LIGHTHORSE TO THE RESCUE

Flying a search and destroy mission nearby, Ace Cozzalio responds to a Mayday call on "Guard" frequency. A Cobra gunship pilot flying cover for the Aviation Company that inserted the Charlie Rangers reports an infantry company pinned down at grid coordinates XS440680.

Flying Crusader Cobra lead, Ace arrives on the scene and begins talking with Norman Prance, the senior RTO hunkered down in front of the bunker. Prance apprises Cozzalio of the situation. He describes the infantry company as scattered in disarray across the open field with many inside the wood line. Most of the dead and wounded are in close proximity to the enemy bunker. Every time the infantry attempts to maneuver, they are cut down by machine gun fire.

Ace tells Prance to hang in there while D Troop takes care of the bunker. Circling the area at five hundred feet, Cozzalio can see Charlie Company scattered across the open area. He locates Prance, pinned down directly in front of the bunker. He is concerned that many of the Charlie Rangers are inside the tree line, making it impossible for the helicopter gunships to attack without endangering the American troops on the ground.

Cozzalio radios the Warwagon Scouts, directing them to attack the bunker. The two Scouts make a couple of gun runs, firing the minigun and M-60 machine gun. They break high over the nipa palms, thinking they have silenced the bunker. Each time, a few minutes pass and the machine gun is active again, firing at the pinned-down infantry.

Ace realizes the bunker must be eliminated, and the best approach is a face-to-face shootout, flying straight into the bunker with guns blazing, something he has done many times before. He calls the lead Scout and tells him to land in an open area about 150 meters east of the woods. Ace lands his Cobra next to the Loach. Rolling the throttle to flight idle, he tells his copilot to climb into the back seat and assume the aircraft commander position.

Ace grabs his gear and walks over to the Loach. After a short discussion with the Scout pilot and his crew chief, Ace trades places with the Scout pilot, who walks over and climbs into the front seat of the Cobra.

On Charlie Company's left flank, Lemons kicks Gulliver's boot and points behind them. Albert Gulliver turns to see a Cobra land next to a Loach about a hundred meters to their rear. Later, he comments, "It was surreal to watch the pilots change places in the middle of a vicious firefight. I had a strange sense that something big was about to happen."

Note: At this point, Charlie Company has been pinned down for almost two hours.

ACE ATTACKS THE BUNKER

Ace climbs into the right seat of the still-idling Loach, fastens his seat belt/shoulder harness, and slips on his helmet. Likewise, his old partner, Specialist 4 William "Wilt" Chamberlain, does the same in the left seat. Cozzalio slowly rolls the throttle to operating rpm while Chamberlain draws the bolt back on his M-60, chambering a round and preparing his machine gun for action. Reaching to the instrument panel with his left hand, Cozzalio flips the minigun "armed-safe" switch to the "armed" position and turns the master selector switch to "fire norm."

Ace calls, "Crusader Three-Eight, Sneaky Snake. I will attack the bunker head on. Follow me inbound, but do not fire. I repeat, do not fire unless absolutely necessary. We have friendly troops in the woods on both sides of the bunker." Crusader 38 (Bob Munhofen) responds, "Roger that. Got you covered."

Ace brings the OH-6 to a momentary hover, lifts the tail, and takes off in a northeasterly direction, over the open plains. Then he makes a tight left-hand turn climbing to about a hundred feet altitude and levels out, returning toward the tree line. Aiming directly for the bunker, he dives the Loach downward at an approach angle of approximately twenty degrees. At this angle, the machine gunner cannot elevate his gun sufficiently to fire at the rapidly approaching aircraft.

Flying fast, Ace passes over the pinned-down infantry and flies directly toward the bunker. Due to the close proximity of the Charlie Rangers, he withholds his fire until he is within thirty meters of the enemy position. Then he opens up with the minigun. Flames shoot out the end of the rotating barrels, and it makes a loud *BRRRRRRRRRRRRRip* sound. The pinned-down infantry troops said later that the electric Gatling-type gun sounded like an extremely loud foghorn as the Loach passed overhead.

With Wilt hanging out the left door firing his M-60 machine gun, the minigun-blazing Loach continues toward the enemy. Emerging from the bunker, two NVA soldiers with AK-47s take a stand in a face-to-face shootout. Ace's aircraft takes several hits in the split seconds before the NVA are blown backward by the massive amount of bullets coming from the Loach.

At precisely the last second, Ace ceases firing the minigun and flares the Loach nose high, coming to a three-foot hover over the top of the bunker. Continuing in one smooth movement, he backs the Loach upward, gaining altitude to about thirty feet. Then he swings the nose downward, diving at the bunker while firing another minigun blast into the open gun ports. *BRRRRRRRRRRRRRip*. At the end of the second dive, Ace lands the Loach on top of the bunker.

Sergeant Mike McClean, aka "Cowboy," manning an M-79 grenade launcher with 1st Platoon, is positioned about fifty meters from the tree line. He watches intently as Ace attacks the bunker. Cowboy tells what happens next. "I see this small helicopter land on top of the bunker and a guy [the gunner] gets out the left side and goes to the back of the bunker. He pulls the pin on a frag grenade and tosses it into the bunker's rear entrance. Then he runs back to the helicopter and jumps in as it lifts off. The grenade explodes with a loud *BOOM* when the helicopter is about eight feet in the air and climbing." Satisfied that the bunker is destroyed, and the enemy is eliminated, Ace lifts high above the woods, banking to the left.

In the newfound silence, the Charlie Rangers give a rousing cheer. The infantry troops are whooping and hollering as Ace swings his Loach in a left-hand turn over the nipa palms.

After the celebration dies down, it is strangely quiet. The remaining NVA in the woods are rapidly retreating. One by one, the brave soldiers of Charlie Company stand to assess the damage. Medics are running to those wounded and needing attention. To everyone's surprise, Norman Prance slowly stands up among the dead and wounded command group. Most thought he was dead as well. Little did they know, Prance was constantly on the radio talking to higher command and Ace Cozzalio, flying above him.

ACE MEETS THE *RTO*

Cozzalio calls Prance on the radio, telling him he is landing his helicopter and will meet him on the ground. He makes his approach and sets his Loach down in the open area about twenty meters behind the infantry troops. He brings the aircraft to flight idle, frictions down the controls, and gets out of the helicopter. Gathering their weapons and gear, he and Wilt walk toward the location of the infantry RTO.

This is a sight to behold for the battle-weary infantry soldiers. They just witnessed a small helicopter wreak havoc on the enemy bunker to their front, and now they see two bold and brazen aircrew approach from the still-running helicopter. The tall, slender guy is wearing a white Stetson cavalry hat. Around his neck, a yellow scarf hangs loosely over his green jungle fatigues. Slung low around his waist is a wide pistol belt with a row of bullets laced around the sides. Attached to his belt is a holstered Colt .357-caliber revolver. In his left hand, he carries a CAR 15 rifle.

In stark contrast, walking next to him is a short, tough-looking guy, carrying an M-60 machine gun with a bandolier of link ammo draped over his shoulder. And, like Ace, he wears a yellow scarf hanging loosely around his neck. What a sight![vi]

Cozzalio and Prance meet in the middle of the open area. Ace commends Norman for doing a great job on the radio and expresses his regret that they lost their commander and other brave soldiers in his company. Together, they walk to the destroyed bunker. Ace is anxious to see what damage he has brought about. There they find the bunker is totally obliterated with body remains of two dead NVA inside and two others in the area outside the bunker.

A short time later, Ace and Wilt walk back to the Loach. Low on fuel and ammo, they take off and return to Dong Tam.

THE BATTLE CONTINUES OVERNIGHT

A short time later, D Company, 5th Battalion, 60th Infantry is inserted on the opposite side of the woods and also engages the enemy. As darkness approaches, three companies from 2nd Battalion, 60th Infantry are inserted, completely encircling the NVA forces in the woods. During the night, Air Force AC-47 "Spooky" flareships and Huey helicopters with xenon searchlights illuminate the area to ensure that the enemy does not escape the trap.

The following morning, U.S. Artillery and Air Force air strikes pulverize the wooded areas. Afterward, the five companies from 3rd Brigade sweep the area, performing a battle damage assessment. At the conclusion of the battle, seventy-eight NVA soldiers are reported killed and a large number of enemy weapons are captured, including eighteen AK-47s, six Chinese Type 53 Carbines,

---

vi   From an audio recording of Ace describing the event to Mike Sloniker in 1993.

three ChiCom PKM machine guns, and seven rocket-propelled grenade (RPG) launchers.[26]

POWs captured during the battle identify the enemy unit as K-6 Battalion, 1st NVA Regiment. The POWs also divulge that the entire 1st NVA Regiment, consisting of three battalions, is operating in the area, preparing for an attack on the provincial capital of Tan An. The attack never happened—the Battle of Phu My was a major setback to the NVA's plans.[28]

On this fateful day, Charlie Company suffered one of their worst enemy engagements in terms of casualties. In addition to the loss of their commanding officer and his junior RTO, 3rd Platoon suffered two dead and sixteen wounded. First Platoon suffered one dead and four wounded, and 2nd Platoon had no casualties. First Lieutenant Hugh Best, the artillery forward observer, died four days after the battle.

In the ensuing battle on the opposite side of the woods, D Company, 5th Battalion, 60th Infantry suffered the loss of Specialist 4 Charles Woodall, who was killed by enemy fire.

SILVER STAR

On the day following the battle's conclusion, Ace Cozzalio is presented a Silver Star impact award (field award) in recognition of his heroic actions on the battlefield.

The 5th Battalion commander is duly impressed. While extending his congratulations, he tells Cozzalio that if he ever wants to command an infantry company to contact him. Ace, being a dedicated cavalry officer and pilot, thanks him for the opportunity and politely declines.

Specialist 4 Norman Prance receives a spot promotion to sergeant. On January 27, Brigadier General William Kraft arrives at Rach Kien to present Prance with a Silver Star impact award for his role in taking charge after Charlie Company's commanding officer was killed. While pinning the award on Prance, the general says, "Sergeant Prance, I can't believe how calm you were during the battle." General Kraft had monitored Prance's radio calls while the Charlie Rangers were pinned down.

DISTINGUISHED SERVICE CROSS

On May 7, 1969, Ace's award is upgraded to the Distinguished Service Cross, and his Silver Star is later rescinded. The award is officially presented to Cozzalio at Fort Knox, Kentucky, while he attends the Armor Officer Advanced Course. In attendance are Ace's mother, Jan, Major Duane Brofer, and Captain Marvin Fuller.

Distinguished Service Cross Presentation
Fort Knox, Kentucky
Courtesy of Rex Cozzalio

CHAPTER 29

FAREWELL

"The gentle art of learning to let go of things is what allows us to meet with the new, to meet with the future."

—ACE COZZALIO

IN THE FINAL DAYS OF May, Ace's Vietnam tour of duty is coming to a close. His official DEROS (date of expected return from overseas) is May 30, 1969. As a general rule, most soldiers pack up and head to Long Binh (Army headquarters near Saigon) for out-processing before this date. Due to circumstances beyond his control, Ace has remained at Dong Tam. His replacement in the role of Crusader Gunship platoon leader has not returned from a two-week R&R, so Ace remains for several days past his DEROS date. Evidently, the 9th Division chief of staff didn't get the message. Upon learning that Ace stayed past his DEROS date, he decided to correct the situation. The following event is unusual to say the least.

ACE IS ESCORTED OUT

Around 0900 hours, on June 2, 1969, Ace is in his hooch, busily organizing his personal belongings. His flying days are over and he is getting ready for his upcoming departure. He is anticipating his farewell ceremony scheduled on the following afternoon, and he plans to depart Dong Tam on June 4, five days past his DEROS.

On a table near his bed, a record player is turning, playing a stack of Ace's favorite albums. As the music plays, Ace sings along with his favorite recording artists: Linda Ronstadt, Johnny Cash, and Aretha Franklin.

Suddenly there is a knock at the door. Ace turns the music off and walks across the room. He opens the door and is greeted by two Military Police officers (MPs) who say, "Captain Cozzalio, you are going home today."

"No, I am not," Ace replies with a laugh, thinking this is a joke. "Who put you up to this?"

The MPs reply, "Sir, we have your orders and they are signed by the division chief of staff," as they hand the papers to Cozzalio. The MPs stand by attentively as he reads the document.

After a long pause, Cozzalio tries to explain his situation, but it soon becomes apparent that the MPs have no latitude and Ace must comply. The two sergeants stand by as he gathers his belongings and packs them into a duffle bag. Then the MPs escort Cozzalio to the flight line, where a Huey is waiting to take him to Long Binh for out-processing and the return flight to California.

When Ace arrives at Long Binh, he calls the Dong Tam SRAO office and talks to Sherry. He laughingly tells her that the MPs escorted him out and he will return soon. Then he heads for the flight line and "hitches" a ride in a Huey back to Dong Tam later that afternoon. He is determined not to let this little detour stand in the way of his farewell and the opportunity to say goodbye.

FAREWELL CEREMONY

On the following day (June 3), Ace is in his room, preparing for his farewell ceremony. While donning his 1860s cavalry uniform—yellow scarf, silver belly Stetson, saber, riding boots, and spurs—he thinks back on the previous eighteen months and is duly proud of his accomplishments. Even so, he has mixed emotions about leaving today—he will miss the camaraderie of the cavalry and the thrill of flying. But, most of all, he regrets having to say goodbye to his friends in D Troop.

Many thought Ace would not leave today, instead thinking he would extend his Vietnam tour another six months. Cozzalio had mentioned extending but never submitted the paperwork. When his friends ask him why he didn't extend, he simply replies that he was busy flying, and time got away from him. Some speculate that when Frank died, the war was over for Ace. He certainly didn't show any emotions in this regard, but his close friends could tell something was awry.

FAREWELL

At 1600 hours, D Troop assembles in three platoons in front of a presentation stand draped with red over white panels of cloth— the cavalry guidon (flag) colors. On the stand are Lieutenant Colonel William Crouch, 9th Aviation Battalion commanding officer; Major Brennon Swindell, Lighthorse commanding officer; Sherry Giles; and two other Donut Dollies.

D troop is called to attention and given the order "parade rest." The troopers stand with legs apart and hands behind their backs. Bright yellow scarves draped around their necks lay loose over green fatigue uniforms. Many are wearing white cavalry hats, while others are wearing Army-regulation fatigue caps.

In front of each platoon, the platoon leader stands at parade rest, his saber drawn with the tip pointed at the ground alongside his right foot. Centered in front of the presentation stand is Captain Ace Cozzalio in his 1860s cavalry uniform, also at parade rest with his saber drawn, pointing to the ground.

Lieutenant Colonel Crouch, wearing an honorary Lighthorse yellow scarf and silver belly Stetson, steps forward and addresses the troop, telling of Ace's many accomplishments in the field as a Warwagon Scout pilot and later as platoon leader for the Crusader Gunships. Then he addresses the legacy Ace imparted on D Troop. He mentions how Cozzalio created the Lighthorse tradition of yellow scarves, silver belly Cav hats, and sabers, and how this tradition instilled a sense of honor and pride in the cavalry that permeated all facets of Lighthorse. This, in turn, created an exceptional level of esprit de corps that was evident to all who interacted with D Troop. This Lighthorse tradition is unquestionably Ace Cozzalio's legacy.

At the completion of the address, Lieutenant Colonel Crouch calls, "Captain Cozzalio, front and center." Ace comes to attention, bringing his saber to the carry position, with the backside of the blade resting in front of his right shoulder. Then he steps forward to the presentation stand, coming to a halt in front of Crouch. Lifting the saber upward, Ace places the saber's hilt in front of his chin in a salute. Then he drops the point to the ground and returns the saber to its scabbard.

Lieutenant Colonel Crouch returns the salute and presents Ace with a silver cavalry spur mounted on a plaque, in recognition of his service with Lighthorse Air Cavalry. Then D Troop is called to "attention" and "present arms." The troopers give Cozzalio a hand salute while the platoon leaders give a saber salute—the ultimate gesture of respect to a fellow cavalryman.

Then, in the distance, a familiar sound is heard—helicopter rotor blades. Moments later, four Loaches and four Cobras make a low pass over the D Troop area, as a tribute to Ace on his departure.

THE PARTY

After the ceremony, the troop gathers in Frank's Fort for a send-off party. D Troop pilots, Donut Dollies, and several pilots from neighboring units gather to party well into the night, extending their goodbye wishes to Ace.

The following morning, Gary Winsett meets Cozzalio at his hooch and together they walk to the flight line. After loading Ace's personal belongings in the back of a Longknife Huey, Cozzalio climbs into one of the jump seats in the cargo area. Winsett climbs into the copilot seat and after cranking the Huey they lift off, flying Ace to Long Binh for out-processing and the return trip to the States.

Ace's combat tour in Vietnam is over. He returns to California on leave and then proceeds to the Armor Officers Advanced Course at Fort Knox, Kentucky.

Ace's Farewell Ceremony – June 3, 1969
Courtesy of Gary Winsett

CHAPTER 30

LIFE AFTER VIETNAM

MILITARY CAREER

ACE HAD A STELLAR TWENTY-YEAR career in the U.S. Army. He was
the exemplary cavalry officer, admired and respected by his commanders and peers as well as the troops he commanded. Captain
Bill Wheeler, who reported to Cozzalio at Fort Rucker, said, "Ace
was undoubtedly the finest commander I worked for and one of
the finest people I have ever known. He was always there for you
when you needed him."

Throughout Ace's career, he upheld the cavalry image. In his office, he had a McClellan cavalry saddle on a stand, and in front of his
desk was a rug in the image of a red and white cavalry flag. Crossed
sabers, a D/3-5 Cavalry flag, horse photos, and cavalry memorabilia
adorned his walls. Instead of the briefcase carried by other officers,
Ace carried saddlebags. When attending military dress functions,
he wore his dress blue uniform with his cavalry saber.

Stationed at Fort Rucker, Alabama, in 1984, Lieutenant
Colonel Ace Cozzalio was commander of the 4th Aviation Training
Battalion. Having attended Command and General Staff College,
it was apparent that he was being groomed for higher command
positions. In 1986, he was recognized in his Officer Efficiency
Report as a "future senior leader of our Army."

Shortly afterward, Ace's career was cut short by medical problems. Experiencing loss of energy, he went to the hospital for

evaluation, and after several tests it was determined he had contracted the Epstein-Barr virus, causing congestive cardiomyopathy. This disease weakens and enlarges the heart muscles, impeding its delivery of blood to the rest of the body. By the time his condition was diagnosed, his heart ejection fraction (amount of blood ejected from the heart) was 28 percent (55 percent or higher is normal).

This news was surely devastating to Ace. Not only was he concerned about his health, but the focus of his entire life was suddenly changed. He never seriously considered any career other than the military. He was dedicated to the Army.

Soon, he came to grips with the new direction in his life. Ace medically retired from the Army on April 28, 1986. He returned to Hornbrook, California, to live on the family ranch. Highlights of his exemplary military career are detailed in Appendix II.

THE RANCH

When Ace tells his family he is coming home, his brother Rex tears down the original one-room cabin where he and his older brother grew up and rebuilds a two-story home on the same footprint. Later, the two brothers expand the home by adding another large room to accommodate Ace's family.

After arriving in California, medical tests report that Ace's heart ejection fraction settled in at 25 percent. Even so, it seems that Ace doesn't show any signs of slowing down. He stays very active and puts all his energy into improving himself physically, spiritually, and mentally.

COWBOY

Living the cowboy life, Ace convinces his brother Rex to join him in team roping. With Rex as the header and Ace as the heeler, they enter many roping competitions. "Between Ace's attitude and his constitution, he was never fatigued," said Rex. "He didn't allow his heart problem to be a factor in his passion for roping. Our performance as a roping team, hoping to earn his 'dreamed of buckle,' may have been disappointing, but we had a great time."

Ace on his horse, Warrior
Photo taken while Ace was attending
Sul Ross University in Alpine, Texas
Courtesy of Rex Cozzalio

Ace and Rex participate in Dennis Reis Horsemanship Classes, learning and refining natural horsemanship techniques. The courses focus on working with the horse's nature instead of trying to control it. It seems Ace's horse doesn't understand the concept and fails the course, much to Ace's frustration. Having as many as seven horses, the brothers have many cross-country family rides and assist with roundups for neighboring cattle ranches.

True to his cowboy lifestyle and his love of western music, Ace and Rex play in a country western band. With Ace on drums and Rex on guitar, they perform at numerous nonprofit events and are popular with the country swing crowd in northern California.

FALLOW DEER

In earlier times, Rex had installed high fences around the inner twenty acres of the ranch to keep out deer. With Ace at the ranch, the brothers discuss various ways to derive income. It is then that Ace suggests, "If you can keep the deer out, you can certainly keep them in. We can raise deer." They agree and initiate the application process for the required state permits.

While the brothers wait for state approval to sell blacktail deer, Ace receives an offer to purchase excess fallow deer from a wildlife park in central Oregon. Native to Europe, these medium-size deer are mostly a spotted chestnut color while the Leucistic species are white. The brothers purchase the small herd of does and bucks, releasing them on the ranch.

Later, after learning that their application for a blacktail deer permit was denied, Ace learns of another opportunity to purchase fallow deer, this time from a different wildlife park in Oregon. Assuming this was a similar herd of mixed does and bucks, Ace purchases the deer sight unseen. After a three-hour trip in his International truck, while pulling a six-horse trailer, he arrives at the park to load the deer. To his surprise, he finds he has purchased a herd of bucks—not a doe to be found. And, to make matters worse, there are no loading pens or ramps. Now this doesn't deter Ace; he grabs his lariat and, to the amusement of the locals, spends the afternoon roping and loading the bucks.

Returning to the ranch, Ace releases the bucks among his herd, even though he realizes having too many bucks will result in infighting. Always seeking to turn a negative situation into a positive, he has the bucks butchered and sells the venison. Tanning the hides with the hair intact, Ace donates the hides to a local Indian tribe for ceremonial purposes since the Indian culture places high spiritual value on a white deer.

Yes, Ace has to suffer a few jokes from close friends about his business plan to raise bucks, but eventually the brothers have a sizable herd of fallow deer on the ranch. They sell venison in the local markets until state regulations limit the distribution process, making the operation unprofitable. The deer are still there today, grazing peacefully behind the tall fence.

COLLEGE

True to his love of music, Ace participates in a jazz band at a local college. It is there that he decides to prepare and teach a course about the Vietnam experience. This course, titled History and Politics of the Viet Nam Conflict, delves into the background of the decisions made before, during, and after the war and the resulting outcomes. He obtains his California Community College Instructor's Credentials and teaches the course at the College of the Siskiyous at Weed, California, from 1988 to 1991.

ELECT ACE

In 1989, Ace ran for Siskiyou County supervisor—District 1. To promote this endeavor, Ace rides his horse well over one hundred miles, campaigning through the vast area of District 1. A large sign is attached behind his saddle that reads, "Elect Ace

Cozzalio, County Supervisor—District 1." A number of people meet Ace at predetermined rendezvous points, delivering food and supplies.

The horseback campaign trip takes ten days. Not bad when you consider that Siskiyou County District 1 consists of 2,633 square miles of rough terrain from the California–Oregon border on the north to beyond Mount Shasta on the south. When the election results are tallied, Ace loses by a small margin.

LIVING MEMORIAL SCULPTURE GARDEN

In 1988, Ace meets two Vietnam Veterans with an unfulfilled vision. Artist Ric Delugo and metal sculptor Dennis Smith have been working to create a Living Memorial Sculpture Garden (LMSG) honoring all who served our country both at war and in peace. Embracing the idea, Ace and a number of other dynamic leaders, most having served in World War II, Korea, and Vietnam, procure the land from the U.S. Forest Service, design the project, and arrange funding for the 137-acre garden.

Located thirteen miles north of Weed, California, on highway 97, the garden sits at the base of Mount Shasta. It consists of larger-than-life-size statues that emotionally touch on the various aspects of war. Volunteers have planted 58,286 trees, one for each American casualty in Vietnam.

Serving on the board of directors for the LMSG, Ace is instrumental in the planning of Phase II, a memorial wall with the names of those serving our country inscribed on marble panels.

ACE MOVES TO PORTLAND

Ace's medical condition gets progressively worse. In 1992, his heart ejection fraction drops to 8 percent. While he has no energy, he never shows any sign of defeat. He is positive and upbeat every day. Working with doctors at a hospital in Portland, Oregon, Ace is put on the list to get a heart transplant. As much as he regrets leaving the ranch, he moves to an assisted-living high-rise apartment complex in Portland, near the hospital, to be ready when a heart becomes available.

While living in Portland, Ace is homesick for the ranch but doesn't allow that to be a factor to drag him down. He fights every tendency to be negative and focuses only on the positive. He meets many people who are, likewise, there for medical reasons, and they all delight in Ace's upbeat disposition and attitude.

Most people living in the facility are seniors, considerably older than Ace, and they call him Colonel. A large group of residents attends a weekly happy hour in the apartment lounge. To everyone's delight, Ace acquires yellow scarves for the attendees and teaches them to sing "Cav songs." It soon becomes a "big event" that everyone looks forward to attending. As always, Ace is true to the cavalry.

Spirit Shirt

Ace is very spiritual, a trait tied to his Indian heritage. His great grandmother, Gramp's mother, was Huron Indian. Before migrating to Oregon, the family homesteaded on the Indian reservation at Red Lake, Minnesota. And, in Oregon, the family interacted with and befriended local Indians. As a consequence, the Indian culture no doubt played a significant part in Ace's upbringing and influenced his beliefs.

While waiting for his new heart in Portland, Ace makes himself a "spirit shirt." This elaborate western shirt, made of buckskin from Cozzalio ranch-raised deer, has fringe along the sleeves and patches symbolizing special events and beliefs in Ace's life.

Ace wearing his Spirit Shirt
Courtesy of Rex Cozzalio

There are patches representing cavalry crossed sabers, Distinguished Service Cross and Purple Heart ribbons, horses, deer, drums, and a waterfall. Imprinted on the sleeve cuffs are "Old Warrior with Special Heart" and "Heart Son of the Lady of the Lake," a reference to Ace's mother, Jan. Under the right arm, a sewed-on sheath with a mountain scene holds an eight-inch stag horn knife.

Carried with the shirt is a small buckskin medicine bag. Underneath an image of a small bird are the following words imprinted on the bag:

A Spirit of
Love
Honesty

Self-reliance
Persistence
Adventure

Wearing his cowboy hat and spirit shirt, Ace is easily recognized. He brings a smile to the face of all who know him and is a beloved friend to all those residing at the assisted-living facility.

HEART TRANSPLANT

At 9:35 p.m. on April 27, 1993, Ace receives a call advising him to report to the hospital. They received a donor heart from a young woman in her twenties, who died in a car accident. Ace calls his brother, Rex, and immediately checks into the hospital.

Ace's mother, Rex, and his wife, Dawn, arrive at the hospital to be with Ace. After the surgery, the heart surgeon approaches them and says, "Ace took this heart better than any patient I ever had. It's a young heart, and Ace will do just fine." Shortly afterward, alarms go off and the nurses come racing by with the crash cart. Ace is in trouble. The doctors assume his body is rejecting the heart. They start giving him powerful drugs intended to repress rejection, but that doesn't work. They continue giving him drugs and keep him almost sedated as his organs are irreparably damaged due to his heart's problems and toxicity of the drugs.

Rex stays with Ace throughout it all and holds Ace's hand. Ace comes to occasionally and responds as Rex talks to him. "You could tell Ace was fighting with everything he had," said Rex. He stays with Ace for eighteen hours. Finally, it is obvious that he is not going to make it, and Rex says, "Ace, you did what you could." Ace dies shortly thereafter.

Ace's Legacy

Ace Cozzalio left a huge legacy, both in the military and his personal life. In the Vietnam War, he was a true hero, putting his life on the line countless times when he attacked the enemy or swooped in to save someone in peril. A number of his fellow troopers can attest that they are here today because of Ace.

In Lighthorse, Ace left the legacy of the yellow scarves and silver belly cavalry hats—a tradition that continues to this day at Veteran gatherings and Lighthorse reunions.

In peacetime, he was a dynamic and inspirational military officer. Exhibiting a genuine "follow me" persona, he never asked his men to do more than he asked of himself. As a leader, he was a mentor to many younger officers and enlisted men, instrumental in the development of the Army's future leaders.

In his personal life, Ace made a lasting impression on everyone he met. He was a cheerful, upbeat, and generous person. He had many friends and would go out of his way to assist or do something nice for those he knew and loved. He had a unique enthusiasm for life that touched all who knew him. This enthusiasm never waned, even when he faced debilitating heart disease.

Ace had a circle of very close friends who were aware of his heart condition and pending heart transplant. They knew him well and were certain that he would, once again, "beat the odds" and persevere. Instead, they all were profoundly shocked and saddened to hear that their good friend had died.

Ace Cozzalio Memorial

On May 5, 1993, a memorial was held for Ace at the Living Memorial Sculpture Garden. Friends and family gathered to remember Ace and dedicate the Memorial Wall, soon to be erected at the south end of the garden.

The following is an excerpt from the dedication speech given by Rex Cozzalio, Ace's brother:

While Ace wisely chose to like himself, with countless knocked over milk glasses, and chandeliers accidentally smashed in the laughing exuberance of the moment, he never pretended perfection, but forever worked to reach it. A real life Hero, he confronted death eye to eye, often outnumbered, over 200 times while defending his loved ones. Yet he could weep at a child's tear and laugh with the beat of his drum.

While not a "traditionally" religious man, he was one of the most spiritual and moral people I have known. And while he has not "always" achieved the goals he set for himself, having been known to rope his own horse's tail on occasion, he always became a greater person for the effort.

If Ace's attitude was his power, then responsibility was his energy. He accepted no less than full responsibility for himself and his actions and expected no less from everyone else. He did not defray to "government" or "others" to "take care of it" but rather looked to the learning, knowledge, creativity and strength we all share to find solutions for ourselves and to a greater world.

We have lost so much with Ace, but how much we have gained. A problem solver, a worker, a leader, and a true visionary, one of his greatest gifts may have been in encouraging others to be greater than themselves. And indeed, who are we honoring this day, if not all of those people who have given so much by being greater than themselves.

In the final minutes of the ceremony, an honor guard was called to "attention" and given orders to fire a twenty-one gun salute. Then a flight of four helicopters passed overhead in the "missing man" formation. As the sound of the helicopters faded in the distance, "Taps" was solemnly played by a lone bugler.

In a final homage to Ace, a riderless, saddled horse with the boots reversed in the stirrups was escorted across the garden by a group of mounted cowboys. Military tradition states that the boots reversed signify that Ace was taking one last look back at his family and the troops he commanded.

HOT LZ MEMORIAL WALL

With the loss of Ace, the board of directors for the Living Memorial Sculpture Garden decided to alter the Memorial Wall project in progress. In memory of Ace, they created a new design and gave the wall a new name: Hot LZ Memorial Wall.

The wall was dedicated on Memorial Day, 1994. In this beautiful setting with Mount Shasta in the background, a large marble wall with two wing panels emerges from the forest floor surrounded by tall fir trees. Each panel is inscribed with the names of those who served our country.

The focal point of the main wall is a tribute to Ace Cozzalio. A large bronze plaque with a life-size bust relief of Ace wearing his spirit shirt and cowboy hat is above a list of his military awards and decorations. Situated on top of the wall is a metal wire-frame sculpture of a Huey picking up soldiers in a "Hot LZ," while a Cobra gunship covers from above—a fitting tribute to Ace.

Hot LZ Memorial Wall near Weed, California

CHAPTER 31

WHO WAS ACE COZZALIO?

WHO WAS THE PERSON BEHIND all those extraordinary accomplishments—the man behind the chest full of medals? The answer is not as evident as a person might assume. Ace was a complex blend of character traits. He was a soldier and a cowboy, mixed with a tad of rock 'n' roll ambition. As a soldier, he was tough and unyielding, constantly seeking to attain his goals and willing to take a risk for the better good. As a cowboy, he was a polite and respectful person who honored both women and children.

Ace was an imposing six-foot-two extrovert with a creative mind and a flair for showmanship. He had a flamboyant personality that endeared him to most, but distanced him from a few. This "larger than life" persona coupled with his confident determination to excel contributed immensely to his success in the military.

THE MILITARY MAN

Ace was a natural-born warrior. In face-to-face confrontations with the enemy, he was seemingly fearless as he charged directly into enemy positions with guns blazing. And, he was a hero. If one of his fellow troopers was shot down or otherwise in peril, he never hesitated as he raced to assist his friend in need.

In 1968, a 9th Infantry Division press release described Ace as an "undisputed king of the air over the Mekong Delta." In that article the author wrote, "Ace, as he prefers to be called, has killed more than 200 enemy. But, as his commanding officer [Major Duane Brofer] is quick to point out, 'on the positive side, think of how many American lives he has saved!'"[18] A good example is that fateful day in January 1969 when Ace hovered his Cobra, protecting the LRRPs, and later flew a Loach to knock out the bunker—rescuing more than ninety American soldiers. On countless other occasions, Ace flew in to save the day for soldiers on the ground or pilots in the air.

After Vietnam, Ace became a consummate cavalry officer, respected and admired by all who knew him. His continual drive for excellence and self-improvement set him apart from his peers. Leading by example, he was widely respected by the troops he commanded and recognized by his superiors as one of the Army's premier commanders. At times, his persistence and never-say-no attitude represented a challenge to his commanding officers. Yet, when the chips were down, there was no one they would rather have leading the troops into battle.

Notwithstanding, there was another side of Ace's character. That side was his care, concern, and love for his family—best revealed in the story of his children.

THE FAMILY MAN

Early in their relationship, Ace and Sherry discussed the importance of children in their lives. They recognized there were many unwanted babies that needed families and, accordingly, they both agreed that adoption would take precedence over having a biological child.

In 1973, while Cozzalio was assigned to a VIP helicopter unit in Bangkok, Thailand, he became friends with a local Thai man who worked in the unit. Over time Ace mentioned that he and Sherry desired to find a baby. Living in Khorat, this man's wife worked in a hospital that had a ward for sick, abandoned babies. Days later, the man approached Ace, telling him that his wife had picked out a baby girl she thought Ace and Sherry would like and set a date for them to visit the ward.

On the agreed-upon date, Sherry and Ace drove to Khorat (160 miles) to meet the little girl. When they arrived they were escorted to a small building with eight babies in cribs. Lifting the little girl from one of the cribs, the caretaker gently placed her in Ace's arms. Another little girl toddled over to Sherry, lifting her little arms in the air. Sherry reached down and picked her up.

Ace's heart sunk as his eyes panned around the room, appalled by all the needy children. He turned to Sherry and said, "We need to take all eight of them. How can we pick one over the other?" He and Sherry both knew that was impossible. How could they make the gut-wrenching decision on which child to save when all were ill and needing medical care?

Then Ace looked down at the baby girl in his arms. She never stopped smiling. Through it all, this child seemed to have the strength and determination to be happy. After some deliberation, they came to a decision. They realized they couldn't save them all, but they could make a difference in the life of this one little girl with the big smile.

After completing some papers, Ace and Sherry left with their baby. As they drove to the American hospital in Bangkok, they realized the baby had no name. They discussed many names as they traveled the road back to Bangkok. As they approached the outskirts of the city they made their decision. They named their little girl Happy.

In the coming months, Ace and Sherry were met with many challenges from the American Embassy and Thai government officials who resisted the adoption. Each objection was met as a new challenge for Ace. True to character, he never accepted "No" as the answer. The week before his tour was over, the Thai government issued the adoption document. With few days remaining, Ace convinced the American Embassy to issue a passport to Chrissa Happy Cozzalio—forever called Happy by her father.

In 1974 while Ace pursued his college degree at Sul Ross University in Alpine, Texas, Ace and Sherry applied and became certified as foster parents. Shortly afterward, they received a call about placing a fifteen-month-old boy, Christopher, with them. They agreed and immediately became attached to this chubby little boy with huge brown eyes. Six months passed quickly and Ace got orders for Recruiting Command in Springfield, Massachusetts. It was then that he learned Family Services would not allow Christopher to leave the state; instead he would be moved to another foster home. Ace met with the district judge in El Paso and, after a lengthy discourse, convinced the judge to direct Family Services to allow Christopher to leave the state. Again, Ace's perseverance won through. Shortly thereafter, Ace and Sherry adopted Christopher.

In 1976, while living in Massachusetts, Sherry gave birth to a baby girl. They named her Cheyenne.

Ace was proud of his children even though his soldierly manner distanced him from his kids at times. After his medical retirement from the Army, he had more time to spend with his children. Giving them horses, he taught them to ride and enjoyed participating with them in local rodeo events. He also volunteered at the high school where all three children attended. Cheyenne, Ace's daughter, commented years later, "My fondest memory of my dad is every day he asked me, 'Have I told you I love you today?' And he always followed up with, 'Well, I do.'"

A glimpse of Ace's true character can be found in his writings. He was fond of making lists—lists of self-development and self-awareness. In his final days, he compiled two lists that revealed his true heart. The first was titled, "What memories fill me with joy?" Grouped together at the top of the list was his horse Cody, D

Troop, and watching his children grow and learn. The other list was titled, "How am I spending the limited number of days that I have left?" The first item on the list was "enjoying my children." If he were alive today, Ace would be enjoying eight grandchildren and one great-grandchild.

CLOSING

In writing this book, I feel I have come to know Ace Cozzalio on a more personal level. He was a highly self-motivated person, always striving to excel and exceed even his own high standards of performance. Having many dreams, Ace wasn't afraid to make mistakes in the pursuit of those dreams, always learning from his endeavors.

In the face of adversity, Ace always chose to take the positive road and never be discouraged by the situation at hand. He was very spiritual, believing a higher force was at play in all walks of life—as evidenced when he wrote, "No one can have anything unless God gives it to him."

Yes, Ace was a colorful, flamboyant person. Yet, he was never boastful of his many accomplishments and he never spoke badly about another person. Instead, he was a kind and generous person, always looking out for those he loved. And, under the steely exterior, beat the warmest of hearts, gentle in ways only understood by his closest friends and family.

But what I admire most about Ace was his childlike enthusiasm for life. He paved his own unique path in the world, yet beneath all the drive and pursuit of excellence, Ace totally enjoyed himself, and that exuberance rubbed off on all who knew him.

Ace was a lot of things to a lot of people, but in his own words he was "Always a Cowboy." So in Ace's characteristic style, I will end this book with the phrase Ace used to close his letters.

Happy Trails

ACE'S AWARDS AND DECORATIONS

Distinguished Service Cross (Inducted into Legion of Valor)
Silver Star
Distinguished Flying Cross (3 Oak Leaf Clusters)
Soldiers Medal
Bronze Star Medal (1 Oak Leaf Cluster)
Purple Heart (1 Oak Leaf Cluster)
Meritorious Service Medal (1 Oak Leaf Cluster)
Air Medal (48 awards, one with V Device)
Army Commendation Medal

Army Achievement Medal
Good Conduct Medal
National Defense Service Medal
Vietnam Service Medal (1 Silver Star and 1 Bronze Star)
Armed Forces Reserve Medal
Republic of Vietnam Campaign Medal
Republic of Vietnam Gallantry Cross with Palm
Valorous Unit Award (1 Oak Leaf Cluster)
Republic of Vietnam Civil Actions Medal Unit Citation Badge (2
Oak Leaf Clusters)
Army Service Ribbon
Overseas Service Ribbon
Master Army Aviator Badge
Air Assault Badge
Cambodian Crew Chief Wings
Expert (Rifle, Pistol)

ACE'S MILITARY CAREER

ARMOR OFFICER ADVANCED COURSE

AFTER VIETNAM, CAPTAIN ACE COZZALIO attended the Armor Officer Advanced Course at Fort Knox, Kentucky. Transitioning from a wartime environment to the classroom was a problem for Ace. He struggled with the core examinations and seemingly had a difficult time attaining the proper attitude for the training curriculum, most of which he had already encountered in Vietnam. His final evaluation stated, "Captain Cozzalio is not recommended for further schooling until such time as his attitude undergoes a drastic change for the better." Years later, Ace looked back on this review and took delight in pointing out how far he had advanced both in schooling and his career.

FORT RILEY, KANSAS

After completion of the Advanced Course, Ace received his first stateside duty assignment at Fort Riley, Kansas and assumed his first command position, commander of D Troop, 1st Squadron, 4th Air Cavalry. In this role, Ace was in his element. He was the ultimate aviation commander, always upholding the cavalry traditions and serving as a superlative example to his troops.

An annual competition was held at Fort Riley to determine which organization would serve the following year as the ceremonial unit and color guard for special functions. An infantry company typically won this competition, and up until that time, no aviation squadron had entered the competition. Ace took the challenge to heart. He selected a group of his sharpest troopers and arranged for color guard training at the airfield. D Troop entered and won the competition, becoming the first aviation squadron to serve as the ceremonial unit for Fort Riley. As a further enhancement, Ace organized the first horse-mounted color guard complete with troopers wearing 1860s cavalry uniforms.

THAILAND

Captain Cozzalio was assigned to Thailand in October 1972 as Rotary Wing Section leader, and later assumed the additional duties of safety officer. In this capacity, Ace directed a training program for Khmer Republic helicopter pilots and also prepared a plan for Department of Army approval, recommending the complete overhaul of the Cambodian helicopter fleet.

Never far from the cavalry, Ace had Wrangler, his appaloosa horse, shipped to Thailand. He set up a cavalry training unit to build camaraderie and instill unit pride.

Attaining his college degree was an important part of Ace's career development as an officer. After being approved for the Army Degree Completion Program, he was told he would receive orders from Thailand to attend the college of his choice.

Ace applied and was approved to attend the University of Southern California to complete a degree in business management. However, Ace the cowboy looked for a college with a rodeo program. He found it in Texas.

College

In 1974, Ace and his family arrived in Alpine, Texas, where he enrolled in Sul Ross University. True to Ace's character, he took calf roping and bull riding classes to fulfill his physical education (PE) requirement. He had a good laugh when he received a letter from the Department of the Army questioning how the cowboy-oriented classes met the PE requirements.

Cozzalio performed well in college. Recognizing his academic excellence and leadership abilities, the business administration faculty selected him to receive the Continental Oil Company scholarship. In August 1975, he received his bachelor's degree in business administration, having attained a 3.8 grade-point average.

Living in Texas had certain advantages for Ace. It enabled him to pursue his cowboy passions; he competed in bronc riding, bull riding, and team roping at rodeos. In later years, he would return to Alpine while on leave from the Army to work on a local ranch—never letting it be known he was an Army officer. They thought he was just another rambling cowboy, dropping in to work the herd.

Recruiting

After college, Cozzalio had a two-year recruiting assignment in the New England area. Once again, he excelled and raised the recruiting standards in the area.

In July 1976, Ace was summoned to Indianapolis, Indiana, to help develop a combat aviation handbook for the Army. This manual, titled *Aeroscout and Observer Tactical Manual,* was based on scout pilot combat tactics developed in Vietnam.

In March 1977, Captain Ace Cozzalio submitted his application to the National Aeronautics and Space Administration (NASA) for training and duty as a space shuttle member. He later received a letter stating that NASA funding had been reduced and there were no openings for new applicants.

GERMANY

Ace was promoted to major in August 1977 and assigned to the 501st Aviation Battalion, 1st Brigade, 1st Armored Division in Katter Bach, Germany. After an interim assignment, Cozzalio became commander of B Company, 501st Aviation Battalion, and served in this position for sixteen months. This was the ultimate assignment for Ace. He was a gifted warrior, and by commanding an attack helicopter company, he was in the role of his lifetime. He demanded excellence from his troops and developed a high level of esprit de corps within his company. His unit had a flawless safety record, and the reenlistment rate was 362 percent of the objective for 3rd quarter, fiscal year 1979.

Ace changed the company name to "B Attack!"—a unique name that clearly defined their combat role and a name his troops were proud to expound. When the Iran hostage crisis occurred in late 1979, he sent a letter to the Pentagon volunteering B Attack! to rescue the fifty-three U.S. hostages held in Iran.

In Major Cozzalio's Officer Efficiency Report (OER), his commander stated, "Best Attack Helicopter company commander in Europe if not the Army! Exciting, dynamic, aggressive, innovative and smart. Boundless enthusiasm. Flabbergasts those who aren't quite as quick. I like his style—others do too, including the allies. A commander's commander! He makes things happen. Better at his job than any I have seen! A warrior. My pick over all the others to prepare a unit and command it in combat. When the time comes, B Attack will kill tanks by the gross. He feeds on challenges and handles them with ease. One of the Army's and aviation's most gifted officers. Destined to do great things!"

COMMAND AND GENERAL STAFF COLLEGE

In June 1980, Major Cozzalio attended Command and General Staff College at Fort Leavenworth, Kansas. He excelled in all areas of the curriculum and was recognized for his enthusiasm, initiative, and dedication to excellence. Upon completion in June 1981, he was promoted to lieutenant colonel.

ROTC

Ace's next assignment was Army ROTC director of instruction at the University of Southern Mississippi in Hattiesburg, Mississippi. There, his leadership and management skills resulted in increased ROTC enrollment from 927 to 1,559 in his first year and to 2,053 the following year. This elevated the detachment to number one in the nation in enrollment. Through his efforts, the ROTC unit passed the Annual Federal Inspection with no major deficiencies and ten commendable areas, all-time highs since 1968. And, true to character, Ace initiated and completed an equestrian center for the university.

FORT RUCKER, ALABAMA

In April 1984, Lieutenant Colonel Cozzalio became commander of the 4th Aviation Training Battalion at Fort Rucker, Alabama, home of the U.S. Army Aviation School. Being an aviator, Ace welcomed the return to Fort Rucker. Like his other assignments, he excelled as a commander and was especially talented in the realm of Army aviation. He was widely known as a soldier-oriented leader who inspired confidence and made things happen.

In October 1984, Cozzalio completed the combat assault, rappelling, rigging, and sling-loading phases of the Air Assault School, thereby earning the distinctive right to wear the Air Assault Badge.

He was the oldest soldier in the class and took great pride in this achievement late in his career.

On April 2, 1985, after having accumulated two thousand flight hours, Ace qualified for his Master Aviator wings—another accomplishment he was proud to attain.

In early 1986, Brigadier General Rudolph Ostovich III wrote in Ace's OER, "Clearly the best battalion commander on post; quite possibly in the entire Army. No wonder his battalion was judged by HQ TRADOC as the best training battalion in the Army. To say he is outstanding in leadership and professional skill does not do justice to his demonstrated performance or potential. He inspires his soldiers to be all they can be. A leader of extraordinary capacity; the perfect soldier role model. Physically fit, technically competent, sincerely committed to the welfare of his soldiers— a warrior. Should be in command of an aviation brigade today. Select for SSC [Senior Service College] soonest so that he can rapidly achieve greater positions of responsibility. A future senior leader of our Army."

MEDICAL RETIREMENT

Having been diagnosed with heart problems, Lieutenant Colonel Ace Cozzalio medically retired from the Army on April 28, 1986, after serving twenty years. He returned to Hornbrook, California, to live on the family ranch.

LEGION OF VALOR

IN 1972, LIEUTENANT COLONEL ACE Cozzalio was inducted into the Legion of Valor of the United States of America, Inc., in recognition of his being awarded the Distinguished Service Cross. This organization, founded in 1890 by Civil War and Indian War Medal of Honor recipients, recognizes and honors personnel who have been awarded the Medal of Honor, the Army Distinguished Service Cross, the Navy Cross, and the Air Force Cross.

The Legion of Valor maintains a museum within the Veterans Memorial Museum in Fresno, California. This museum tells the story of America's wars from the perspective of the recipients of the nation's highest awards. This facility houses thousands of items donated by Legion of Valor members and others. A large display case is dedicated to Lieutenant Colonel Ace Cozzalio. It contains his Army green uniform, medals, plaques, and a photo of Ace in his 1860s cavalry uniform.

Ace Cozzalio Display
Legion of Valor Museum

ACE'S NOTES

BEFORE HIS SURGERY, ACE PREPARED handwritten cards addressed to each of his closest friends. He asked his mother, Jan, to send the cards, regardless of the outcome of the surgery. In Ace's characteristic style, the cards leave his loved ones with an image of how he wished to be remembered.

Howdy,

I have had my heart transplant.
Everything is going GREAT!
I am on my way back to riding in the saddle again.
Thank you for all your love and support.
I will write more in a week or two.

Happy Trails,
Ace

His mother added the following to each card before mailing:

Ace had addressed this card to you prior to entering the hospital. I was to notify you when he stabilized.

"Ace is stable, happy and busy organizing the Mystical Warriors into a Cav Unit. Today—as always—he soars as an eagle—and no bird soars too high if he soars with his own wings."
Remember him & smile. He loves you.

Mom Jan

LIGHTHORSE CHARGES ON

THE 9TH INFANTRY DIVISION "OLD Reliables" redeployed to the United States in August 1969. Left without a parent organization, D Troop was reassigned and attached to the 7th Squadron of the 1st Cavalry Division operating out of Vinh Long Army Airfield, thirty-eight klicks (twenty-four miles) west of Dong Tam on the Mekong River. Arriving in Vinh Long in January 1970, Lighthorse continued to operate as a separate and distinct cavalry troop and further reinforced the "Bastard Cav" image.

SWAPPING GUIDONS

In January 1971, for reasons unknown, the Army exchanged unit designations between two air cavalry troops. No personnel were moved and no equipment was relocated—only the unit numerical designations were traded.

Overnight, the two troops swapped guidons (swallow tail unit flag displaying troop, squadron, and regiment numbers). Lighthorse went from D/3-5 Air Cavalry to the new designation of C/3-17 Air Cavalry. At Quang Tri in I Corps, the northernmost corps in Vietnam, Charlie Horse went from C/3-17 to D/3-5. They exchanged letter and number designations of troop, squadron, and regiment—no other changes were made.

Lighthorse Troopers continued to wear their yellow scarves and silver belly Stetsons. The troop insignia and uniform patches were changed to C/3-17, leaving the Lighthorse, Longknife, Crusader, Warwagon, Doughboy, and Scavenger identifications and call signs intact.

Lighthorse Stands Down

In early 1972 Lighthorse received stand-down orders, and in April C Troop 3rd of the 17th Cavalry folded its colors. The troop guidon was sent to Squadron Headquarters at Di An to rejoin the other 3-17th troops as they, likewise, stood down and departed Vietnam in April 1972. This event marked the last time that yellow scarves and silver belly Stetsons were worn by an active cavalry troop. The Lighthorse legacy had come to a close, leaving many troopers with fond memories of their time with the "Bastard Cav."

Lighthorse Troopers with at least six months service in Vietnam were redeployed to C Troop, 3rd of the 4th Cavalry, stationed at Schofield Barracks, Hawaii. Those with less than six months were reassigned to other units in Vietnam.

Later, the 3rd Squadron of the 17th Cavalry was officially inactivated on June 19, 1973, at Fort Lewis, Washington.

3-17TH CAVALRY REACTIVATED

On June 2, 1988, 3rd Squadron of the 17th Cavalry was reactivated as the cavalry squadron of the 10th Mountain Division (Light Infantry) at Fort Drum, New York. The 3-17th Cavalry deployed to Florida as part of the relief efforts following the disastrous Hurricane Andrew in 1992. A few months later, the squadron deployed to East Africa as part of Operation Restore Hope in Somalia. There the Squadron conducted reconnaissance and security operations to assist in restoring order to the famine-stricken country.

LIGHTHORSE RETURNS

In October 2003, the 3-17th Squadron deployed to the Middle East in support of Operation Iraqi Freedom. It was there that the Lighthorse name reemerged when the 3-17th Squadron became Task Force Lighthorse, attached to 3rd Brigade, 2nd Infantry Division, the Army's first Stryker brigade on its initial operational deployment.

The Task Force was comprised of:

* Redhorse Troop (HHT/3-17)
* Blackjack Troop (B/3-17)
* Crazyhorse Troop (C/3-17)
* Blue Tiger Troop (D/3-17)
* Voodoo Company (A/2-10 AVN)
* Diamondback Company (C/1-10 AVN)
* Viking Company (C/10 AVN, AVIM)

The Lighthorse Task Force and its troops were vital in the success of daily ground missions, providing aerial reconnaissance and security throughout AO North. The 3rd Squadron, 17th Cavalry Regiment served with valor in Operation Cyclone, Operation Blizzard, Operation Mayfield, Operation Valiant Saber, and Operation Resolute Sword. After a highly successful deployment, the task force redeployed back to Fort Drum in December 2004.

In 2008, as part of a restructuring of the Combat Aviation Brigades, the 3rd Squadron, 17th Cavalry was relieved from assignment to the 10th Combat Aviation Brigade, 10th Mountain Division and reassigned to the 3rd Combat Aviation Brigade, 3rd Infantry Division. The squadron was stationed at Hunter Army Airfield, Georgia.

LIGHTHORSE TODAY

As an element of the 3rd Combat Aviation Brigade, 3rd Infantry Division, the 3-17th Squadron's mission is to, on order, deploy worldwide and provide security and reconnaissance operations in support of the 3rd Infantry Division. The 3rd Squadron, 17th Cavalry Regiment is comprised of six troops:

* Headquarters and Headquarters Troop (Redhorse) provides communication, medical, ground maintenance, logistical support, and Command & Control for A, B, C, and D Troops.
* A Troop (Silver Spurs), B (Blackjack), and C (Crazyhorse) Troops operate OH-58D Kiowa Warriors equipped with a variety of weapons and surveillance systems to provide air security and reconnaissance for the squadron and division.
* D Troop (Blue Tigers) provides maintenance operations on OH-58D Kiowa Warrior aircrafts, to include airframe,

armament, avionics, and electrical systems; downed aircraft recovery and repair; and technical supply operations.

﹡ E Troop (Sabre) deploys worldwide to conduct ground sustainment operations in support of the squadron or task force during combat operations.[29]

Recent Deployments:
OPERATION IRAQI FREEDOM—Baghdad, Iraq (2007–08)
OPERATION ENDURING FREEDOM—Jalalabad, Afghanistan (2009–10)
OPERATOIN ENDURING FREEDOM—Kandahar, Afghanistan (2012–13)

Acknowledgments

I WOULD LIKE TO THANK all the people who graciously helped with this project by providing their stories and information. Without their assistance, this book could never have been written.

Lighthorse Troopers
Lorin Bliss
Duane Brofer
Don Callison
Robert Campbell
David Conrad
Carl Eisemann
Jim Flynn
Marvin Fuller
Mike Galvin
Eloy Garcia
Bob Grove
Johnnie Hanks
Johnny Hutcherson
Randy King
Ken Lake
Ray Lane
Jack Lerch

Larry Loftis
Don Matthews
Brock McCloskey
Hubert McMinn
Bob Munhofen
David Newkirk
Chuck Nole
Tom Nutting
Rich Petaja
Mike Rasbury
Bob Schultz
Les Smith
Quinn Sowell
Brennon Swindell
Rick Waite
J.B. West
William (Whit) Whitworth
Gary Winsett

Ace's Friends and Family
Cheyenne Cozzalio
Christopher Cozzalio
Rex Cozzalio
Lynn Hayes, 210th &, 70th Avn
Chrissa Happy Cozzalio Kvist
Hugh Mills, B/8th Avn (Attack)
Mike Sloniker, A/501st Avn
Sherry Cozzalio Taylor

Friends of the Project
Randy Baisden, F-4 Cavalry
Dwight (Bud) Beck, C/4-47 Inf
Mark Brockway, E/2-60 Inf
John Conway, VHPA Museum
James Howard, Sr., 1st Cavalry
Jim Lehne, 2-60th Infantry
Gary Linderer, 101st, LRP/Rngr
Phil Marshall, 237th Med Det
Tom Norton, 44th Med Bde
Maj. Gen. Rudolph Ostovich III
Ron Quesada, HHC & B/3-5 Cav
Gary Roush, VHPA Database
Jim Shepard, 50th Infantry
Jim Thayer, E/50th Inf LRRPs
USAF Pararescue Association

The "Brothers" of Charlie Company 5th Battalion, 60th Infantry
Bob Cooper
Leonard Cowles
John Depko
Richard Desper
Albert Guillorn
Albert Gulliver
Gene Jackson
Pat McAloon
Mike "Cowboy" McClean
Norman Prance

GLOSSARY

AC—Aircraft commander

AGL—Above ground level

AK-47—Soviet 7.62-caliber assault rifle with thirty-round curved magazine

AMC—Air mission commander

AO—Area of operations; i.e., mission area

ARVN—Army of the Republic of Vietnam; i.e., South Vietnamese Army

Ash & trash—Noncombat mission carrying ammo, supplies, or personnel

Autorotation—Descending maneuver where the helicopter engine is disengaged from the main rotor system and the rotor blades are driven solely by the upward flow of air through the rotors. Nearing the ground, pitch (angle) is increased in the rotor blades, resulting in a normal landing.

AWOL—Absent without leave

Backseat—U.S. advisor and ARVN counterpart riding in the passenger compartment of the Command & Control Huey helicopter

Bubble—Curved Plexiglas windshield

Bunker—Fortified fighting position, generally dug into the ground with gun ports for shooting

C&C—Command & Control helicopter, typically a Huey

CAR 15—AR-15 assault rifle with collapsible buttstock; carbine version of the M-16 assault rifle

Cav—cavalry

Cav Team—Two Scouts and two Gunships accompanied by a C&C aircraft

Chalk—Flight position. Chalk one is the lead, chalk two is the second position, chalk three is the third, etc.

Charlie—Nickname for Vietcong, derived from phonetic alphabet: Victor Charlie

Charlie Model Huey—Specially developed gunship version of the "B Model" Huey. It incorporated the upgraded Lycoming T53 engine and the new Bell 540 rotor system.

Chicken plate—Heavy chest protector body armor made of aluminum oxide ceramic covered with cloth

Chin bubble—Plexiglas window near the pilot's feet allowing visibility of the ground in front of the helicopter

Chinook— Twin-engine, tandem rotor heavy-lift helicopter. Its primary roles are troop movement, artillery placement and battlefield resupply.

Chieu Hoi—Vietnamese for "surrender"

CO—Commanding officer

Cobra—Bell AH-1G helicopter gunship; replaced the Charlie Model Huey gunship

Collective—Control stick on the left side of the pilot. Lifting the collective increases pitch (angle) in the rotor blades for lift. On the end of the collective is a motorcycle-like grip that controls power to the engine. The collective controls the vertical movement of the helicopter.

Commo—Communications

Cyclic—Stick between pilot's legs that controls left–right and forward–backward movement of the helicopter. Essentially, the cyclic control tilts the rotor disk in the direction of desired movement.

DEROS—Date of expected return from overseas. A soldier's expected day of departure from Vietnam.

Dink—Disparaging term for a North Vietnamese soldier or Vietcong

Donut Dolly—Women working for the American Red Cross in Vietnam

Dustoff—Emergency patient evacuation of casualties from a combat zone. Dustoff helicopter was a specially equipped Huey fitted with stretcher racks and emergency medical supplies.

FAC—Forward air controller; Air Force propeller-driven aircraft used for tactical air support and fire direction

Flechette—One-inch-long, fin-stabilized nails that look like small metal darts. Flechettes are housed within 2.75-inch Hydra-70 rockets. Fired from Cobra gunships, each rocket disburses approximately 2,200 flechettes together with a red puff of smoke to mark the release point.

Free-fire zone—Area where any person is deemed hostile and a legitimate target by U.S. forces

Gook—Disparaging term for a North Vietnamese soldier or Vietcong

Grunts—An affectionate name given to infantry soldiers

GIs—American soldiers. This term originated during World War II and was derived from "Government Issue."

Guard—Emergency radio frequency monitored by aircraft in Vietnam; 243 MHz UHF or 121.5 MHz VHF

Guidon—Swallow-tailed troop flag and mast denoting troop, squadron, and regiment letters and numbers. Cavalry guidons are composed of a field of red in the upper half above white in the lower half.

Guns—Gunships

Gunship—Helicopter with heavy armament, such as rockets, minigun, and/or grenade launcher

Ho Chi Minh sandals—Sandals worn by the Vietcong. The soles were made from tire tread, and the straps were cut from inner tubes.

Hooch—Slang term for a place to live, either a soldier's living quarters or a Vietnamese hut. The most typical hooch was a thatched-roof dwelling.

Hot extraction—Helicopters pick up troops on the ground while receiving hostile fire

Huey—Bell UH-1H utility helicopter carrying six to eight soldiers and gear; manned by a crew of four, two pilots, and two door gunners

Intel—Intelligence reports

IV Corps—Southernmost military quadrant in Vietnam, comprised mostly of the Mekong Delta

Klick—Military slang for kilometer (.62 miles)

Line formation—Tactical formation with soldiers walking abreast toward the enemy

Loach—Hughes OH-6A Light Observation helicopter, also called a Scout

LOH— Light observation helicopter, see Loach

Lost his cherry—The first time the pilot's aircraft took hits from enemy fire

LRRP—Long-range reconnaissance patrol; primary mission is reconnaissance with no direct contact with the enemy

LZ—Landing zone

M-16—Colt 5.56-millimeter assault rifle carried by U.S. troops

Medevac—Medical evacuation, typically by helicopter

Mic—Microphone

Minigun—Six-barrel, 7.62-millimeter rotating barrel, Gatling-type machine gun, capable of firing two thousand or four thousand rounds per minute

MPC—Military Payment Certificate, a form of currency to pay U.S. military personnel in foreign countries

MRF—Mobile Riverine Force

N_1 speed—Speed of the first compressor fan in the Lycoming turbine engine

Nails—See Flechettes

Nam—Slang for Vietnam

Newbie—Slang term for new guy

NVA—North Vietnamese Army

Oak Leaf Cluster—Worn on medal to denote subsequent awards. Bronze denotes one award and Silver denotes five awards.

O-Club—Officers' Club

OCS—Officer Candidate School

OER—Officer Efficiency Report

OPS—Operations Center, the flight planning office

Patrol formation—LRRP term: trail formation with point man in front, team leader, RTO, rifle man, rifle man/asst. team leader, and drag man with radio

Pax—Aviation terminology for passengers

Pedal turn—While at a hover, the pilot, using the anti-torque foot pedals, turns the helicopter's nose left or right, rotating the helicopter on its vertical axis.

Peter pilot—Slang for copilot

Push—Slang for radio frequency

PRC-25—Backpack squad radio carried by infantry RTOs

PRC-90—Handheld survival radio. Operated on 121.5, 243, and 282.8 MHz AM. It had a beacon mode, and a tone generator to allow sending of Morse code.

PSP—Perforated steel planking used for runways

PX—Post Exchange

PZ—Pickup zone

R&R—Rest and recreation. A soldier's vacation from the war. Typically two weeks during a one-year tour in Vietnam.

Recondo—Reconnaissance tactics taught by Army Rangers to include patrolling, land navigation, weapons, and survival techniques

Revetment—A barricade protecting against explosives; commonly, a four-foot-high, L-shaped wall protecting helicopters on the flight line

ROTC—Reserve Officers' Training Corps

RPG—Chinese Communist rocket-propelled grenade fired from a shoulder-held launcher

RTO—Radio telephone operator

SKS rifle—Soviet-designed Simonov semi-automatic 7.62-millimeter rifle. It has an effective range of four hundred meters.

Slick—UH-1 Huey helicopter without rockets or heavy armament

Snake—Cobra gunship

Sniffer—Apparatus to detect human activity by sensing odors

Sortie—A group of helicopters assembled for a single attack or insertion of troops

Spider holes—A camouflaged one-man foxhole; typically a shoulder-deep, round hole, covered by a camouflaged lid, in which a soldier can stand and shoot

Spooky flareship—AC-47 (Douglas DC-3) aircraft dropping parachute flares to illuminate the battlefield at night

Squadron—Unit containing four troops, typically an air cavalry unit

Tour—Tour of duty; one year in duration, unless extended

Trail formation—Each helicopter following one behind the other, with each successive aircraft stacked slightly higher in altitude

Translational lift—Mode of flight where the helicopter transitions from hovering "ground effect" to actual flight. Additional lift is created by horizontal flow of air across the rotor blades.

Troop—Cavalry unit with approximately two hundred troopers

VC—Vietcong

VR—Visual reconnaissance

Willie Pete—White phosphorus, used in grenades and rockets. It burns fiercely and can ignite cloth, fuel, ammunition, and other combustibles.

Wingman—Trail aircraft in a pair, responsible for covering the lead aircraft

WO—Warrant officer; a military rank above the highest enlisted rank and below the lowest officer rank, addressed as "Mister"

Wobbly one—Warrant officer 1, rank 1 of 4 possible ranks

WWAS—War wagon air strike

XO—Executive officer

References

[1] Eastman, David, *Outlaws in Vietnam: 1966-67 in the Delta*, (Portsmouth: Peter E. Randall Publisher, November 1, 2001), 3

[2] Truong, Lt. General Ngo Quang, *The Easter Offensive of 1972* (Fort McNair: U.S. Army Center of Military History, 1977), 137

[3] Hinds, James W., "Third Squadron, Fifth Cavalry Vietnam—Part I, Fifth Cavalry Legacy," 1992, accessed May 14, 2014, http://3-5cav-blackknights.org/history/Unit%20History%20Part%201.pdf

[4] Anon., "A Typical Day in Lighthorse 1969," Unit Introduction Briefing given to Vinh Long AAF commander and 7th of the 1st Air Cavalry Squadron commander, December 1969, accessed October 15, 2014, http://www.lighthorseaircav.com/d-unit-organiz69.html

[5] Zahn, Randy, *Snake Pilot: Flying the Cobra Attack helicopter in Vietnam*, (Dulles: Potomac Books, September 30, 2003), 35

[6] Anon., "Narrative Mission Report," (6-38-67-12 Dec 67), Detachment 6 of the 38th Rescue and Recovery Squadron, Bien Hoa, December 12, 1969

[7] Howard, James B., "Flying Circus—Scouts," HHC, 1st Brigade—1st Cavalry Division (Airmobile), Republic of Vietnam, accessed July 20, 2014, http://www.flying-circus.org/reflections/Scouts-JH/Scouts-JH.html

[8] Mills, Hugh L. Jr., *Low Level Hell* (Novato: Presidio Press, 2000), 76

[9] Smith, Richard P., "From Covered Wagons to Warwagons, D Troop, 3d/5th Armored Cavalry," *Octofoil Magazine*, 9th Infantry Division in Vietnam, Vol. 1/Oct, Nov, Dec 1968/No. 4, 9–12

[10] Inman, Jack, "The People Sniffer," 4th ID Chem, Camp Enari, Pleiku, RVN, accessed July 24, 2014, http://www.angelfire.com/ga3/galkie/Sniffer.html

[11] Viet, Ha Mai, *Blood and Steel, South Vietnamese Armor and the War for Southeast Asia* (Annapolis: Naval Institute Press, 2008), 38–39

[12] Davis, Charles G., "CAMP COOPER," Handbook of Texas Online, Published by the Texas State Historical Association, accessed July 18, 2014, http://www.tshaonline.org/handbook/online/articles/qbc09

[13] McWaters, Mike, "Manufacturers of Regulation Model Swords During the US Civil War," accessed July 29, 2014, http://www.angelfire.com/wa/swordcollector/marks/page1.html

[14] Anon., "LOH pilot yanks two from downed chopper," *Ninth Infantry Division—The Old Reliable*, Vol. 2, No. 36, September 19, 1968

[15] Army Helicopter Loss Report, UH-1D 66-00937, Incident number: 680819221ACD, Accident case number: 680819221, 08/19/1968

[16] Holloway, Warren, "Copter Pilot—Home on Leave—Says Vietcong Are On The Run," *Sacramento Bee,* December 25, 1968, D2

[17] Anon., "Dong Tam—United Hearts and Minds," Vietnam Tour 365 website, accessed August 1, 2014, http://www.gingerb.com/vietnam_dong_tam.htm

[18] Smith, Spc. 5 Richard P., 9th Infantry Division Press Release, September 1968

[19] Bradley, Doug, "Donut Dollies Deserve Our Thanks," *Huffington Post*, March 28, 2012, accessed June 20, 2014, http://www.huffingtonpost.com/doug-bradley/donut-dollies_b_1384233.html

[20] Grau, Regan Jay, "Waging Brown Water Warfare: The Mobile Riverine Force in the Mekong Delta 1966–1969." (Graduate School M.A. Thesis, Texas Tech University, 2006) 1–2

[21] Mesko, Jim, *Riverine: The Brown Water Navy in Vietnam*, 1986, accessed June 14, 2014, http://www.mrfa.org/mrf.htm

[22] Loomis, Larry, Specialist 4, "4-47th, Support Units Kill 92 VC," *Ninth Infantry Division—The Old Reliable*, Vol. 3, No. 22, June 4, 1969

[23] Hunt, Ira A. Jr. *The 9th Infantry Division in Vietnam: Unparalleled and Unequaled* (Lexington: University Press of Kentucky, 2010), 138

[24] Findlayson, Colonel Andrew R., "A Retrospective on Counterinsurgency Operations." Central Intelligence Agency Library, 2008, accessed December 22, 2014, https://www.cia.gov/library/center-for-the-study-of-intelligence/csi-publications/csi-studies/studies/vol51no2/a-retrospective-on-counterinsurgency-operations.html

[25] Linderer, Gary A., *Phantom Warriors II* (Presidio Press, 2001), accessed October 14, 2014, http://ichiban1.org/pdf/Memorial/PhantomWarriorsII.pdf

[26] Lafield, First Lieutenant Bill, "3rd Bde Traps, Kills 78," *Ninth Infantry Division—The Old Reliable*, Vol. 3, No. 5, February 5, 1969, 1

[27] Anon., "5-60 RTO Assumes Command During Fight in Plain of Reeds," *Ninth Infantry Division—The Old Reliable*, Vol. 3, No. 6, February 12, 1969, 3

[28] Hunt, Ira A. Jr., *The 9th Infantry Division in Vietnam: Unparalleled and Unequaled*, (Lexington: University Press of Kentucky, 2010), 118

[29] "3rd Squadron, 17th Cavalry Regiment 'Light Horse,'" GlobalSecurity.org, accessed October 13, 2014, http://www.globalsecurity.org/military/agency/army/3-17cav.htm

INDEX

Made in United States
Orlando, FL
14 February 2023